Canal Linocuts
along the
English & Welsh
Canal System

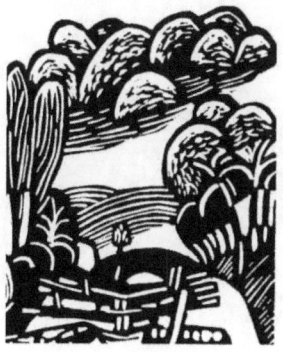

Eric Gaskell

Text
Paul Higson

2023

ISBN 978-1-4092-9745-1

FOREWORD
by Tony Lewery

The subject of canals and waterways has appealed to many different artists over the last couple of centuries, increasingly so as the years go by and their original conception and design becomes part of a romanticised past. The original romantics of the canal age had some difficulty in seeing them that way, for canals were then new, brash and mainly seen as part of the pollution of an increasingly industrial age. The Lake District was fine, or a Scottish castle by a loch, but the inky waters of Birmingham or the waterside mills of Manchester had to wait a while for their pictorial magic to be appreciated. Nostalgia is only part of the modern story however. There is the actual grace of the architecture of that time and now the real patina of age, the history of wear and repair of a working transport system. It is a record on the landscape of thousands of working lives and millions of tons of cargo carried in boats and barges, now conveyed to us in bricks and bridges and a peaceful water channel. How can a modern visual artist tell something of that story with honesty, without dipping into wistfulness?

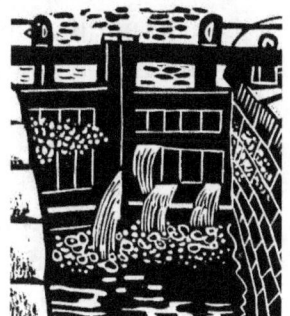

I

Eric Gaskell is an artist, marking down clear visual statements. He is also a neat hand-craftsman and he has chosen the medium of linocut prints to offer us his new look at canals, a fresh eye on the architecture and engineering and the landscape they pass through. It is a process that needs a skilful combination of hand and eye, of craftsmanship and vision. Each mark of a lino print is hand-made, cut in with a knife, engraved, gouged, drilled or scored into the surface of the lino block to create a white mark when it is inked up and printed, a negative mark in the positive printing surface. The process of reducing the myriad details of reality to a crisp image suitable for the linoblock needs careful visual distillation, a decisive analysis of the key elements that need to be included. The material itself also has a bit of a mind of its own, guiding what's possible and creating happy accidents and the resulting artworks are a combination of these many factors. But top of the list is Eric's artistic judgement and balance, the style in which he presents this selection of canal scenes, the way he manipulates the stonework, the arches and lock beams. But still the essence of the real scene remains.

All these prints work well as abstract compositions, interesting arrangements of contrasting textures, strong lines and bright whites, wriggling nature interacting with the man-made order of the canal structure. Eric's work pulls the two together, pushing growth patterns into the brickwork and formalising trees and clouds into nature's architecture. Each scene has a liveliness of its own and a good-humoured vitality. Try looking at any of them upside down and they still have that abstract visual power – sparkling rhythms, dancing sunlight, swooping curves, stately bars and steps marching up the page. Try it.

But each print is actually a record of a recognisably precise place, some iconically well known to the canal traveller like Stoke Bruerne or Chirk aqueduct, others less so like Dean Locks near Wigan. Rather fittingly for the transport subject each picture is something of a journey in itself, from an exploration of the gravel or bricks underfoot, past the lockbeams and bridges, leading us into a sunlit and generally hopeful distance. Perspective may be pushed and planes flattened for the pattern making but Eric's translation of each scene through the medium of the linocut print presents us with a whole new set of images, however familiar some of these places are to the canal enthusiast. For the uninitiated they are an invitation to explore the world of waterways, to join the friendly trees peeping over the hedge or the battalions of Eric's cupid clouds cavorting in the sky. OK, let's go and explore.

Tony Lewery
Ellesmere
2009

The Plates

The lino prints reproduced in this book are from a limited edition and are smaller than actual size. Most of the originals are 105mm x 150mm in size.

THE ANDERTON BOAT LIFT WAS reopened in 2002 after nearly twenty years closure caused by the corrosive salty Cheshire environment. However the lottery funded 'restoration' leaves it looking nothing like the original elegant 1875 structure, and operating differently than it had in the eighty years before closure! The large sloping tubes were added as strengthening in 1905 when it was converted from hydraulic to electric power, along with hundreds of tons of counterweights, gears, pulleys and beams. The lift is now hydraulically powered again, but much of the additional ironwork has been retained for 'historical reasons'.

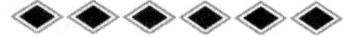

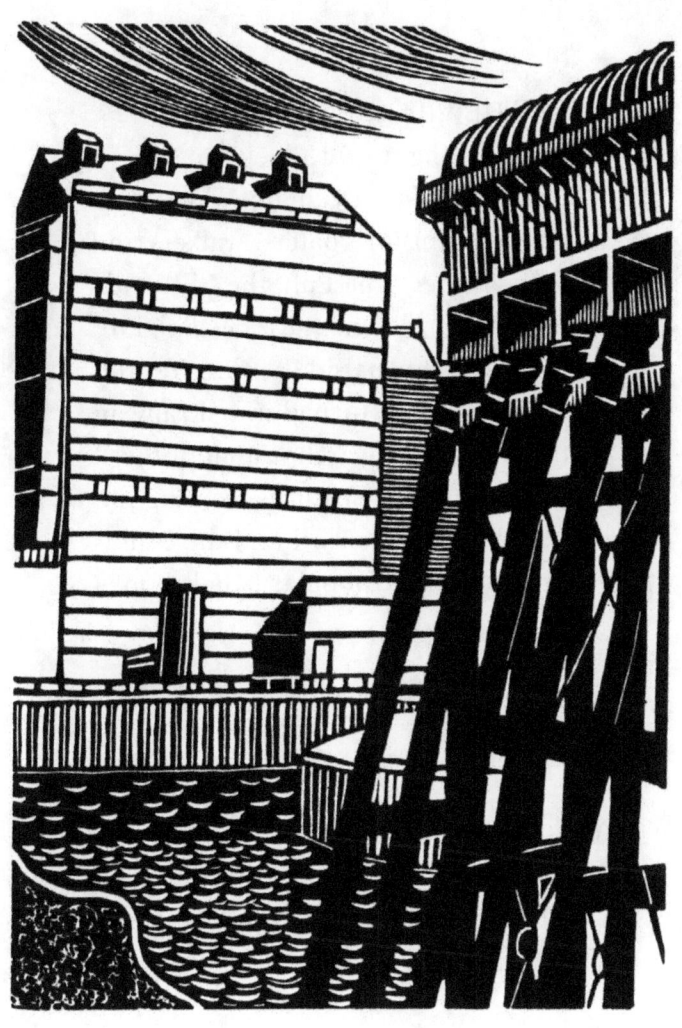

ANDERTON LIFT & RIVER WEAVER

THE VILLAGE OF AUDLEM
with its flight of 15 locks on the
Shropshire Union Canal is a popular
stopping point for boaters, walkers and
other visitors. The Pub, the Mill and
the signature crane have become an
almost iconic canalside setting. Yet the
canal was almost turned into a railway,
the Pub was a warehouse until the
1970's, the crane spent its working life
in a railway goods yard and the Mill is
a pioneering & popular canal shop!

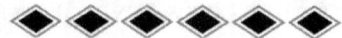

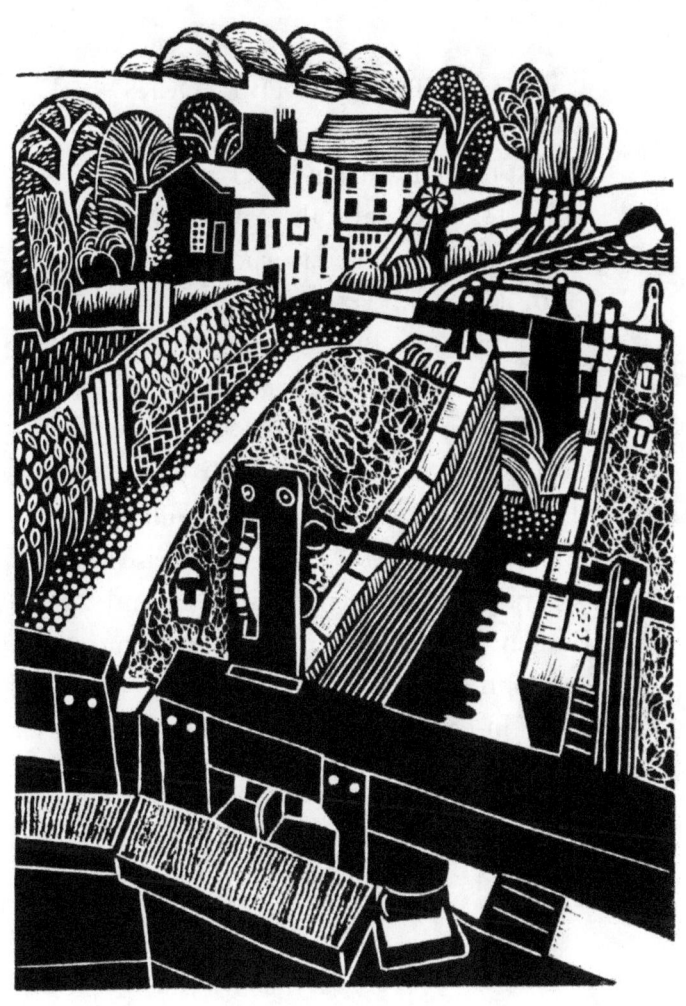

AUDLEM MILL, THE SHROPPIE FLY & LOCK 13

THE STAIRCASE OF FIVE LOCKS
at Bingley in West Yorkshire, the
largest of eight massive lock staircases,
which together raise the Yorkshire side
of the Leeds and Liverpool Canal
47m[155ft] to the Pennine summit near
Littleborough. Bingley Five Rise lifts
the canal 18m[60ft] in a distance of just
97.5m[320ft]. The staircases were
designed by canal engineer John
Longbotham of Halifax and built by
local stonemasons. The 3 two rise
staircases, 4 three rise staircases and
Bingley Five Rise were an engineering
triumph of their day, opened in 1774
in ceremonies watched by
an estimated 30,000 people.

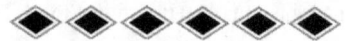

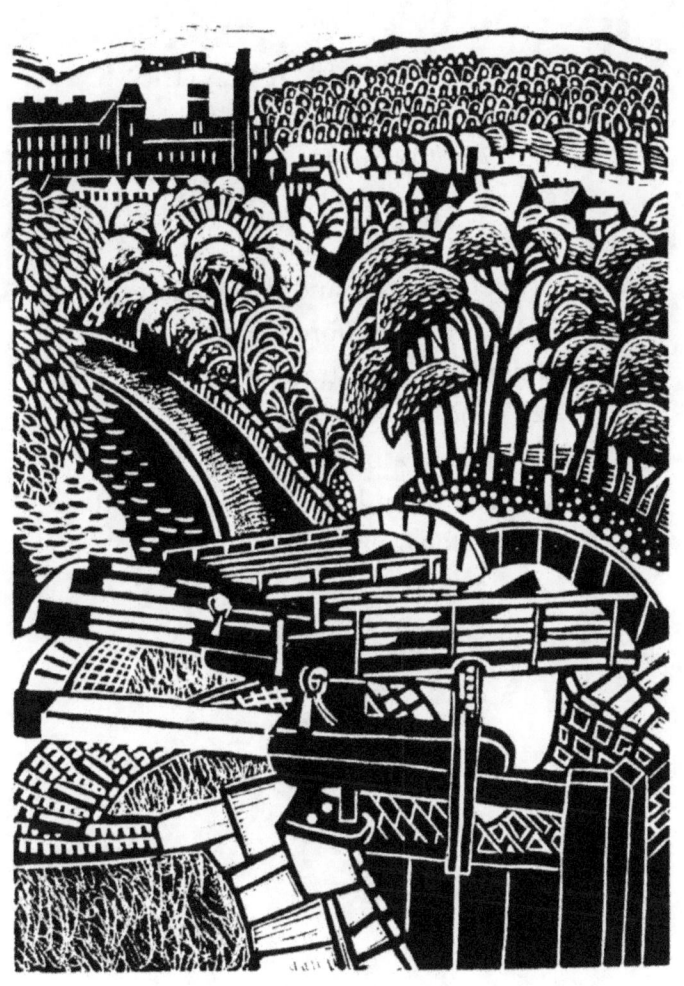

BINGLEY FIVE RISE

BRAUNSTON'S 18TH CENTURY
dry docks sit across the original line of
the 1774 Oxford Canal, where the
Grand Junction Canal joined it in
1805 to create a more direct line
between London and the Midlands.
When the Oxford Canal was
modernised and straightened in the
1820's the old junction was bypassed
and became a boatyard where canal
boats have been built and maintained
for over 200 years.

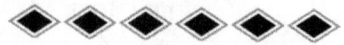

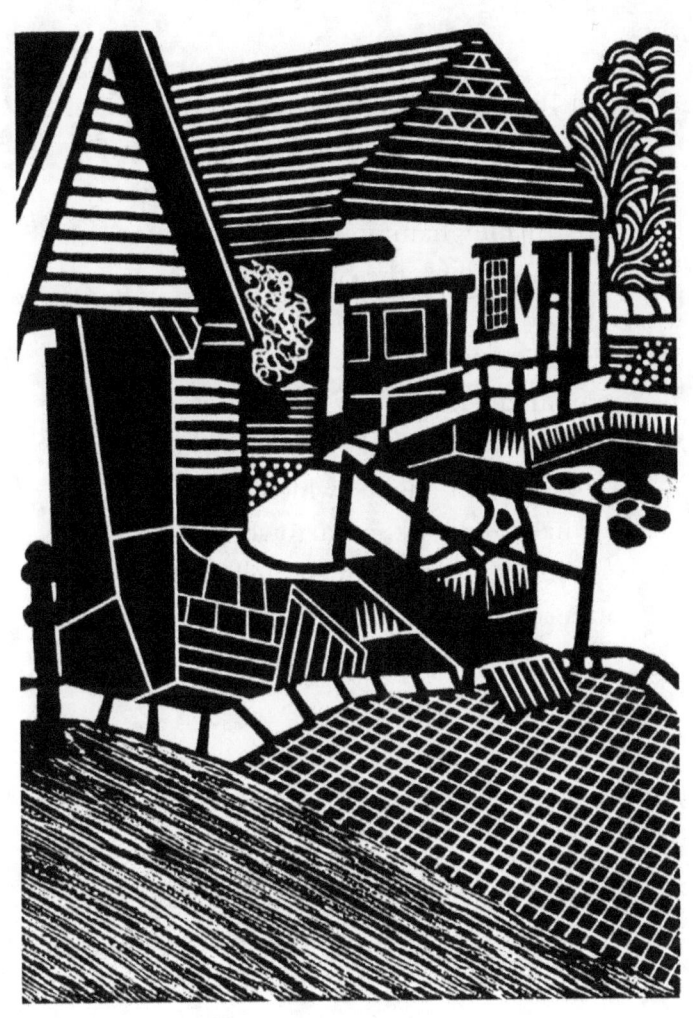

BRAUNSTON DRY DOCKS

BRIDGE 78 SITS AMONG THE FLIGHT of 15 locks at Audlem, part of Telford's plan to build a canal more like a railway. His Birmingham and Liverpool Junction Canal, later the Shropshire Union Canal, slices through hills in deep cuttings and strides over valleys on high embankments, taking the straightest and quickest route. Locks were bunched close together in 'flights' which made them quicker to work; a narrowboat locking through most Audlem locks can be entering one lock while hauling its butty into the lock behind.

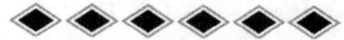

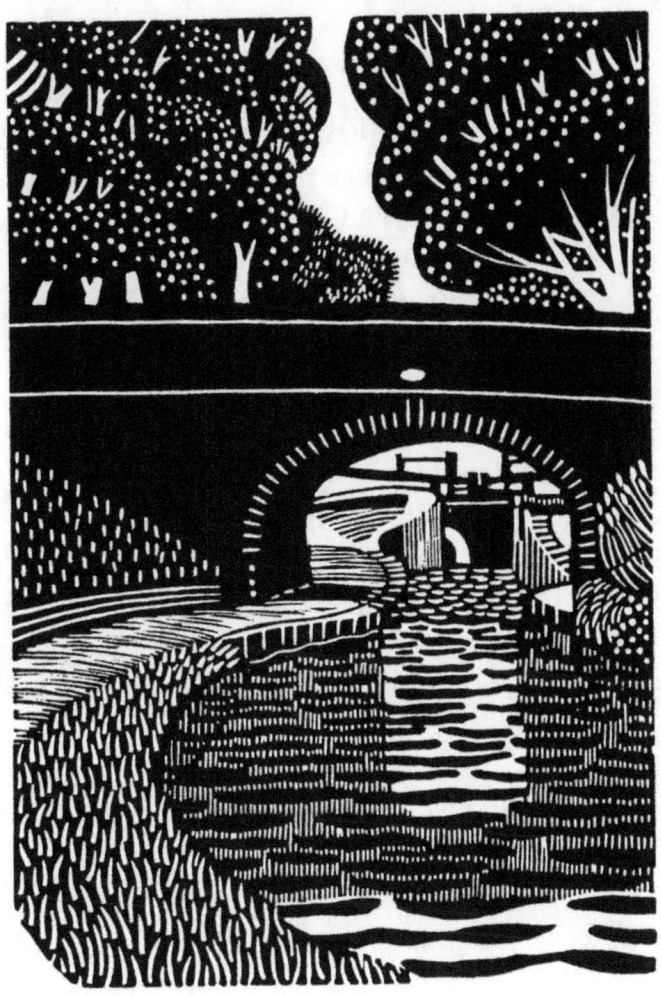

BRIDGE 78, AUDLEM

CASTLEFIELDS IN THE CENTRE of Manchester lies at the junction of the Duke of Bridgewater's Canal and the Rochdale Canal. There are restored wharves, fine warehouses and revitalised city centre open spaces, but most impressive are the Victorian cast iron railway viaducts which soar over the basins, most still used by local trains and Metrolink trams. The castle turrets on the far viaduct were an attempt to blend in with the historic nature of the site, controversial even then because the railways and canals obliterated a Roman site.

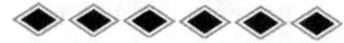

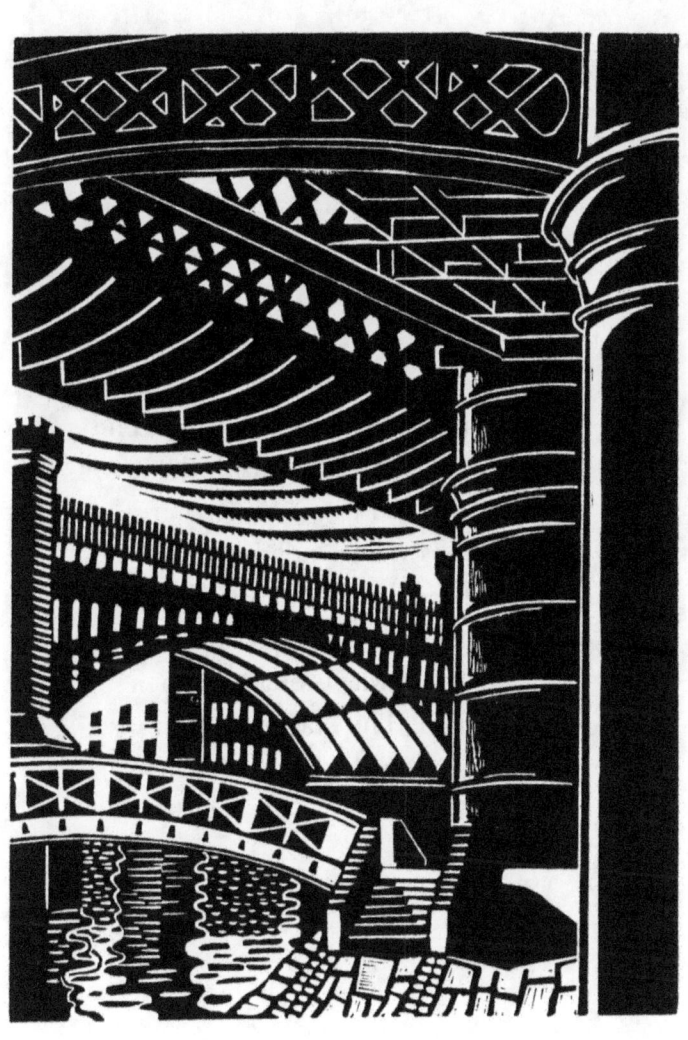

BRIDGEWATER CANAL, MANCHESTER

BUGSWORTH BASIN WAS ONCE
one of the largest and busiest inland
ports on the narrow canals, a unique
interchange where limestone and
gritstone from Derbyshire quarries was
transshipped to narrowboats. Closed in
1927, it was reopened in 2005 after 30
years of hard work by volunteers. The
view shows the Middle Basin, the arm
on the left led to a wharf where
narrowboats were loaded with burnt
lime. Straight ahead is the Upper
Basin and the Silk Hill bridge down
which silk was brought from
Macclesfield. The Navigation pub is
on the left.

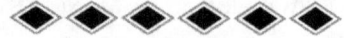

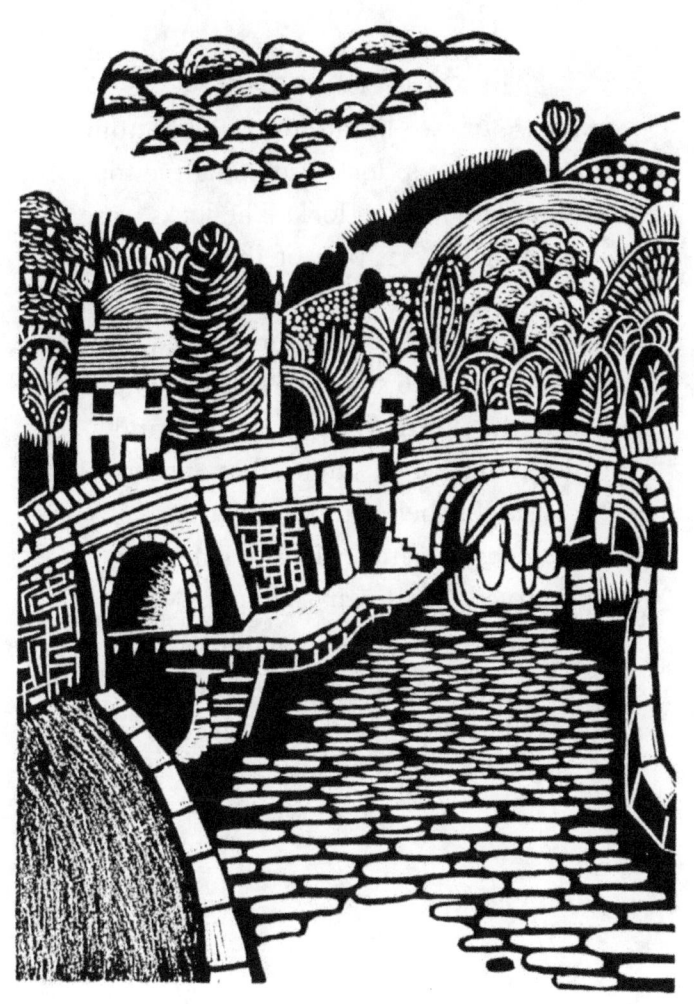

BUGSWORTH BASIN

BUNBURY LOCKS ARE A
staircase of two broad locks, the bottom
gates of the top lock also being the top
gates of the bottom lock! The locks were
built in 1777 as part of the Chester
Canal from Chester to Nantwich. This
became part of the Shropshire Union
Canal in 1846, creating a new route
from the North West to the Midlands
canal system. The stables that once gave
overnight shelter to the boat horses,
ponies and mules have been well
preserved. Most canalside pubs would
have provided overnight stabling for boat
horses. Stables also provided
replacement horses for the fast
Shropshire Union 'fly boats'.

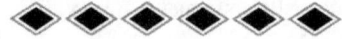

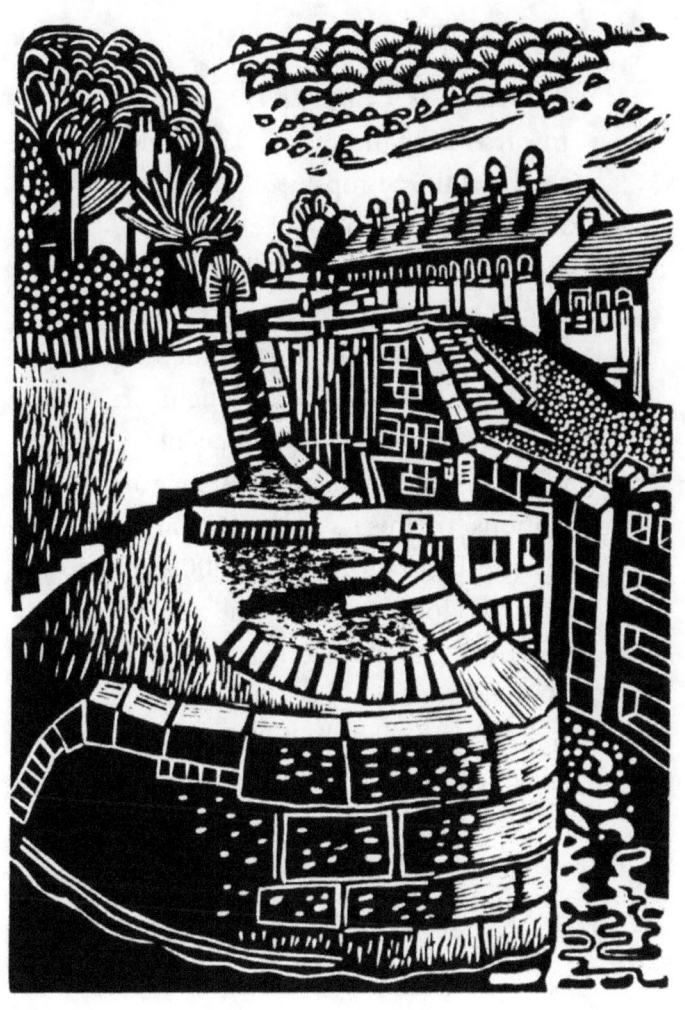

BUNBURY LOCKS

CHIRK AQUEDUCT LOOKING
towards England on the Llangollen
branch of the Shropshire Union Canal
was built between 1796 and 1801 by
Thomas Telford and William Jessop.
The canal is carried in a cast iron
trough which is hidden inside the
masonry, almost as if the engineers
were not confident of their new
material. The 'bold civil engineering
solutions' of this stretch of canal won
it World Heritage status in 2009. The
railway viaduct stands 10m[33ft] higher
the work of the Scottish engineer
Henry Robertson in 1846-8 (rebuilt
1858) and carried the GWR mainline
from Birkenhead to Birmingham.

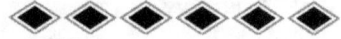

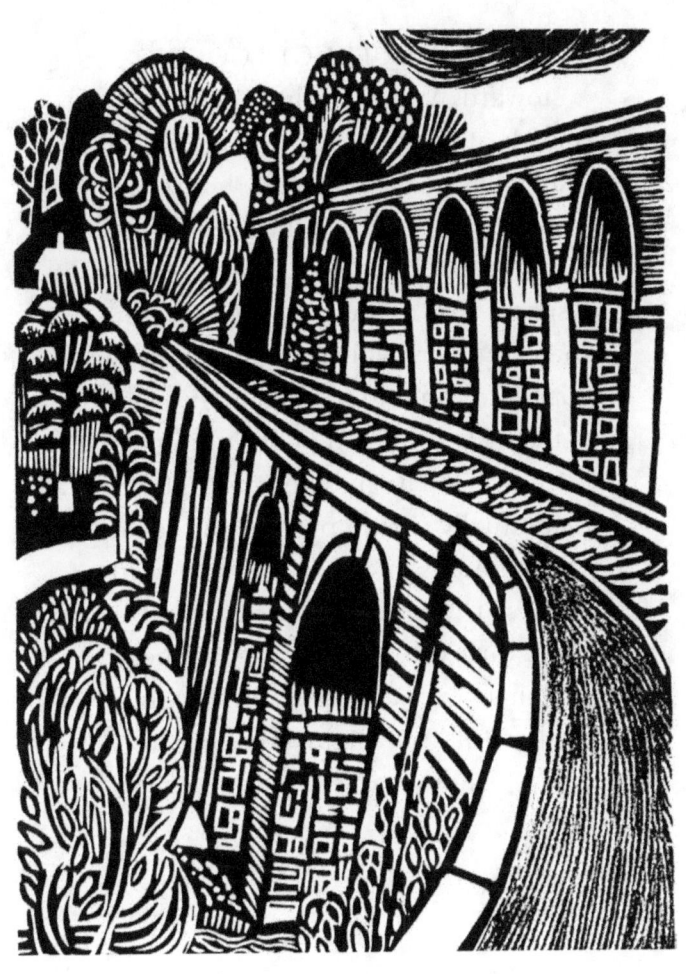

CHIRK AQUEDUCT LOOKING TOWARD ENGLAND

CHIRK AQUEDUCT LOOKING
towards Wales on the Llangollen
branch of the Shropshire Union Canal
carrying the canal across the Ceiriog
Valley 20m[65ft] below. The ten circular
masonry arches of the structure each
span 12m[40ft] and are supported by
masonry piers which are hollow at the
top. The canal immediately dives into
the 421m[1381ft] long Chirk Tunnel,
proof of the hilly terrain which
eventually was to prevent the canal
reaching its intended destination in
Chester. World Heritage Status was
awarded to 17.7km[11mls] of the
Llangollen Canal describing it as a
'feat of civil engineering of the
Industrial Revolution'.

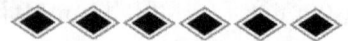

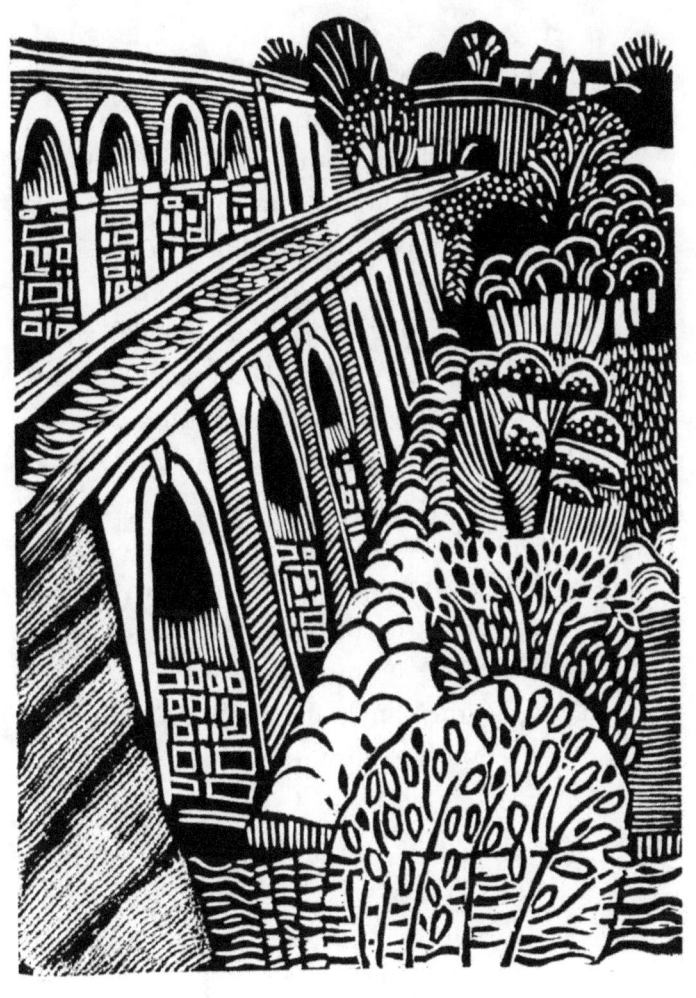

CHIRK AQUEDUCT LOOKING TOWARD
WALES

DEAN LOCKS AT GATHURST
were built in 1774 large enough to fit
river barges from both the Mersey and
Humber, although it was to be forty
years before that trans Pennine route
was complete. They are close to the
start of the long climb that takes the
Leeds and Liverpool Canal off the
Lancashire Plain and over the
Pennines into Yorkshire, 92 locks in
all. The modern girder bridge is the
six span Gathurst Viaduct, completed
in 1963, carrying the M6 motorway
soaring over the Douglas Valley, into
which are crammed the River
Douglas, the canal, and the Wigan to
Southport railway line.

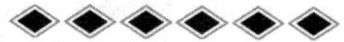

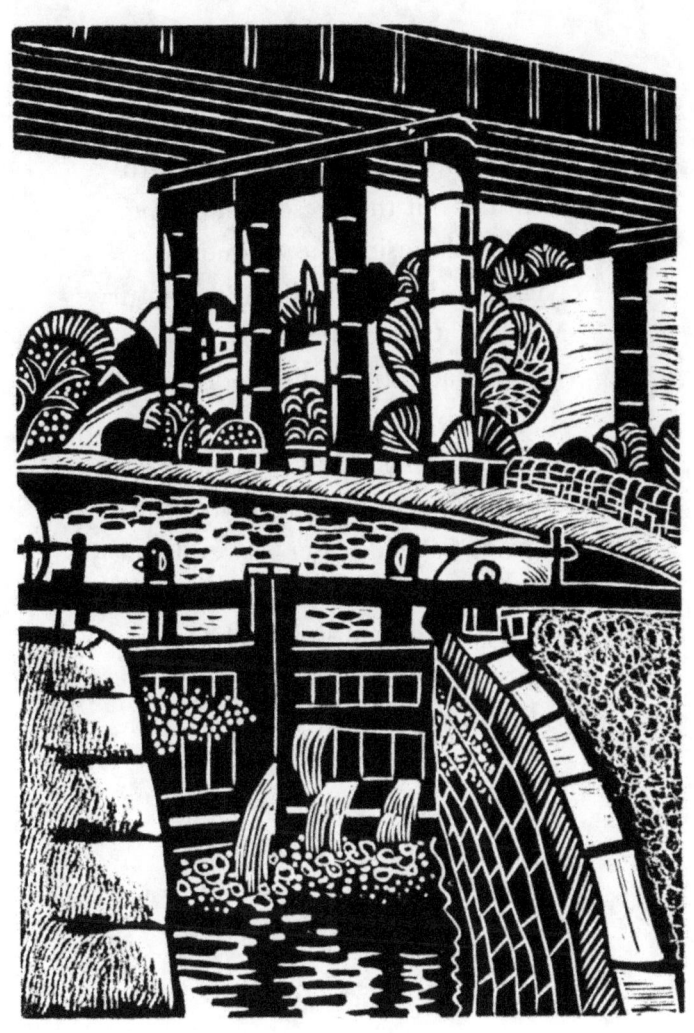

DEAN LOCKS, GATHURST

EBLEY MILLS HAVE SAT IN THE
Stroudwater Valley since the 14th
century, but the present imposing
blocks alongside the Stroudwater
Navigation date from the 19th century.
Much of Gloucestershire's historic
wealth came from the wool trade,
originally based in cottages in hilltop
towns, moving down into the river
valleys when Industrial Revolution's
factories needed water power. Once
there were over 200 mills but falling
demand and competition left most
unused by the mid-20th century.
Stroud District Council now occupies
Ebley Mill.

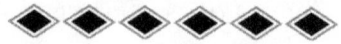

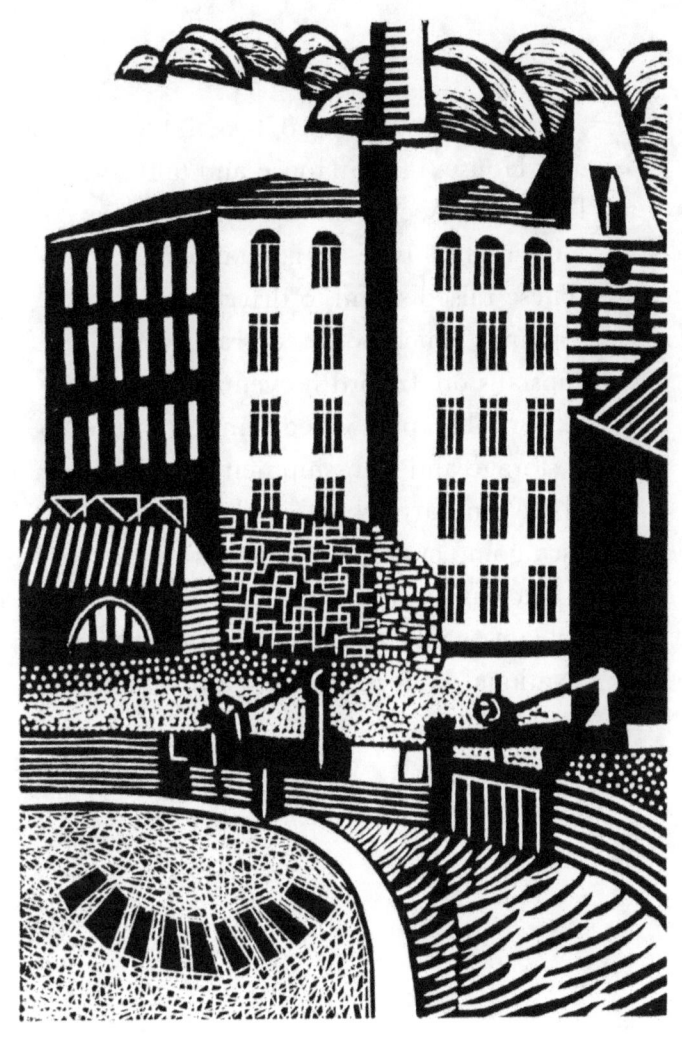

EBLEY MILLS, STROUD

THE ADJOINING 1876 BOILER
House, Pump House and tall
Hydraulic Accumulator contained two
Lancashire type horizontal boilers.
These raised steam to drive hydraulic
pumps which powered cranes and
capstans on Telford's seven acre canal
port. The port was an important
storage and transshipment facility
between narrowboats and river and
sea going craft. One boiler is still in
place and can regularly be seen in
steam as part of the exhibits at the
National Waterways Museum which
now covers the site.

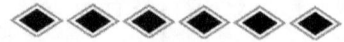

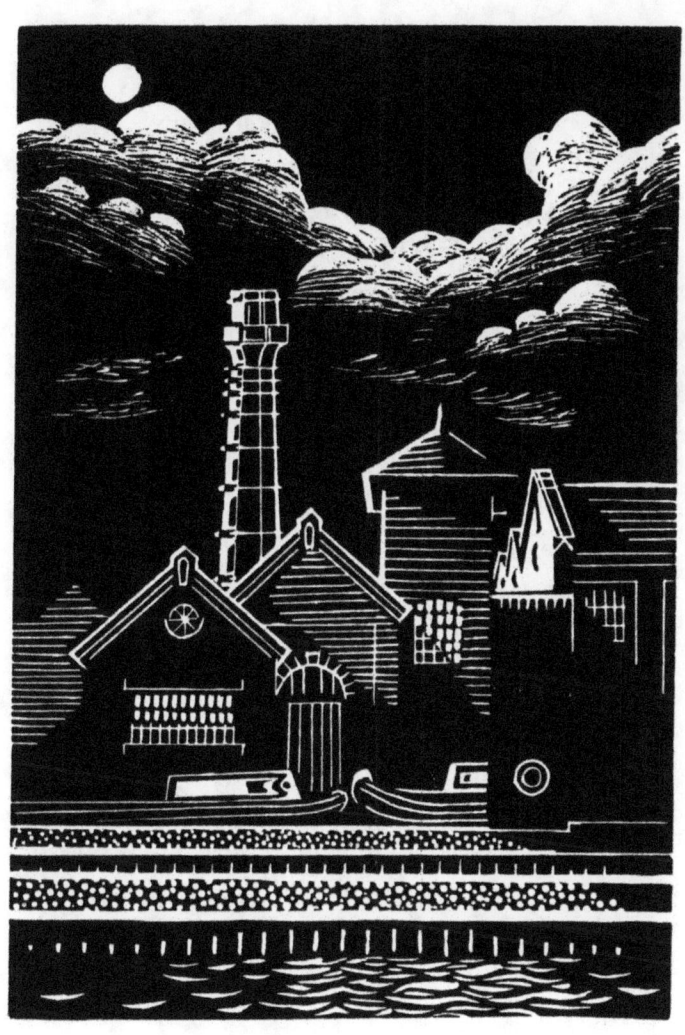

Ellesmere Port Pump House

FARMERS BRIDGE LOCKS IN
Birmingham. Birmingham is 61m[200ft]
above the surrounding countryside and
was being bypassed by the early canals
which were intent on linking the
Rivers Trent, Mersey and Severn
using as few locks as possible. But
merchants funded a short canal to
serve local coalfields and then the
Industrial Revolution created a
network of over 290km[180mls] of canals
and 216 locks. The 13 Farmers Bridge
Locks lift canals from the East and
Southeast up 24.7m[81ft] to the level of
Telford's 'New Main Line'.

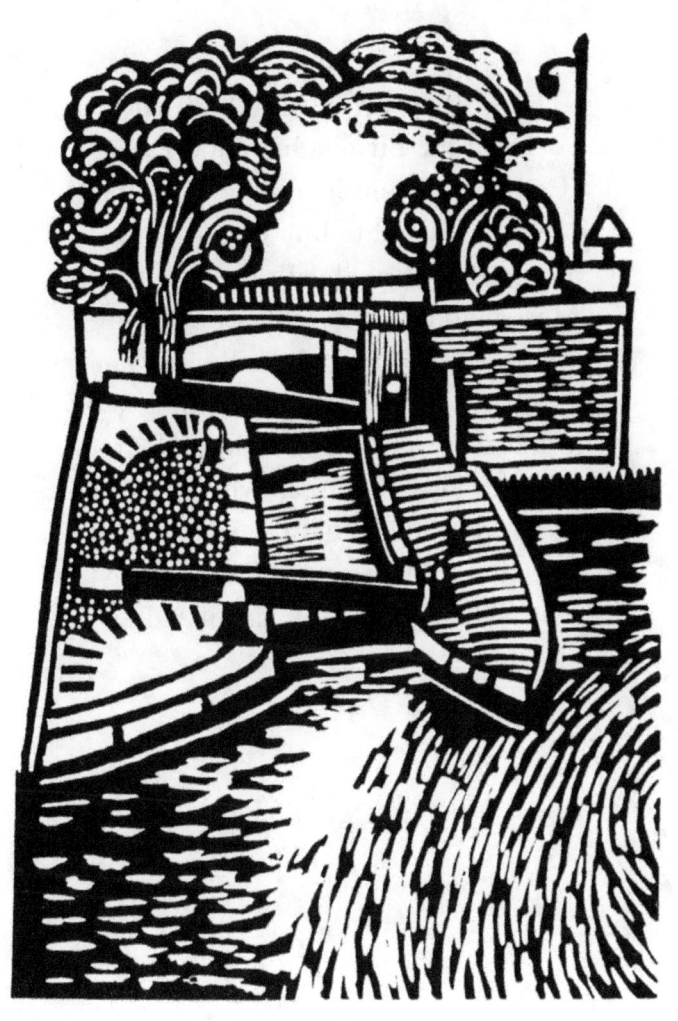

FARMERS BRIDGE LOCKS I

THE THIRTEEN FARMERS BRIDGE
Locks on the Birmingham and Fazeley
Canal were built in 1787. The canal
was intended to link the original
Birmingham Canal with the Trent and
Mersey and Oxford Canals, providing
a link to London and the South. The
locks became so busy that lighting was
installed for 24 hour working. The toll
house can still be seen where boats
were 'gauged' so that the weight they
carried could be measured and the
tolls they must pay calculated.

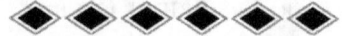

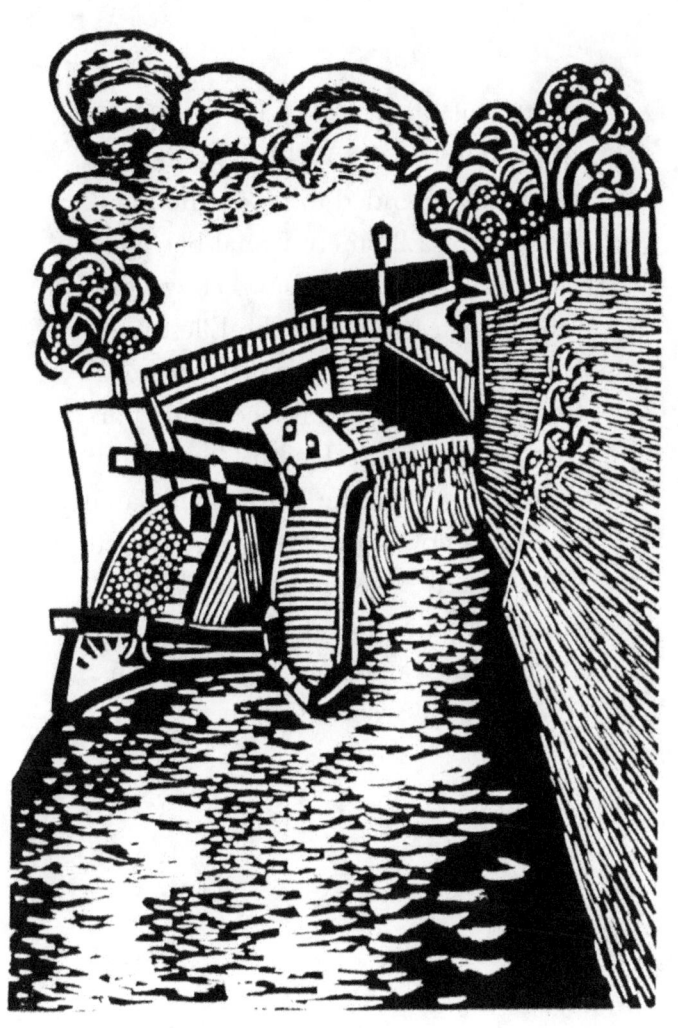

FARMERS BRIDGE LOCKS II

THE FOUR LOCKS AT FRANKTON, Shropshire on the Welsh border were originally intended to be on the main line of the Ellesmere Canal between Chester and Shrewsbury. However money was short and the Ellesmere canal reached neither Chester nor Shrewsbury, eventually becoming part of the Shropshire Union Canal, and what we now call the Llangollen Canal. The locks now stand at the entrance to the 61km[38mls] Montgomery Canal which was abandoned after a breach in 1944 but is undergoing restoration towards Newtown.

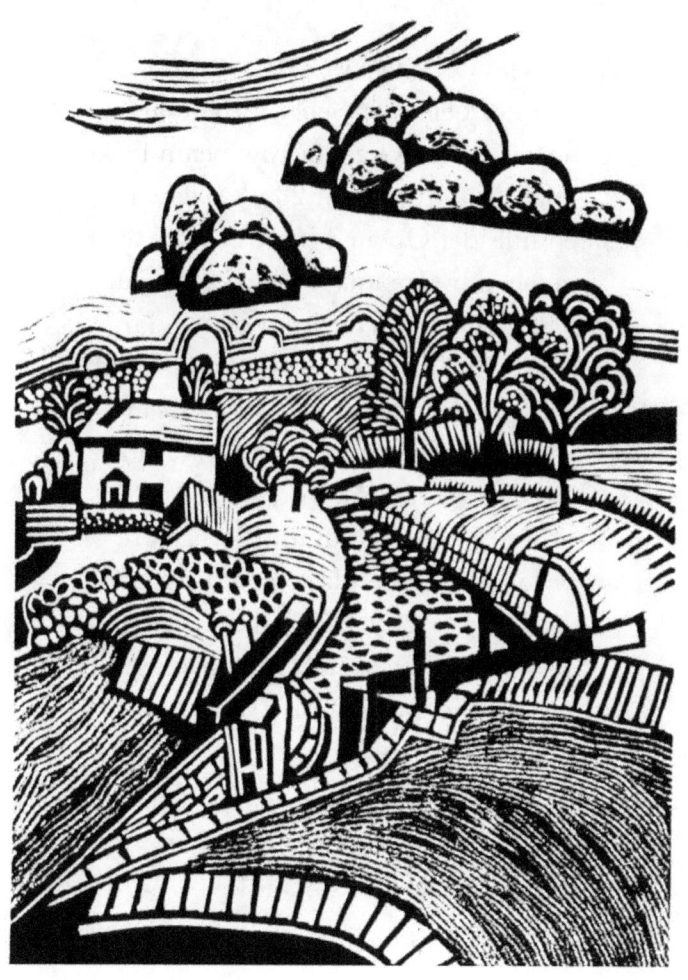

FRANKTON LOCKS

AT FOXTON ON THE GRAND
Union Leicester Section there are
two staircases of five narrow beam locks
which drop the canal 23m[75ft] down a
steep hillside. Opened in 1814 they were
replaced by Foxton Inclined Plane in
1900. The plane consisted of two large
tanks which were winched up a slope
and were able to take wider craft in a
fraction of the time with no water loss.
However as the Watford Locks at the
other end of the summit level were
never widened the plane could never be
used to capacity and high operating
costs resulted in its closure and reuse of
the locks from 1911.

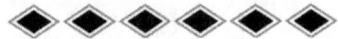

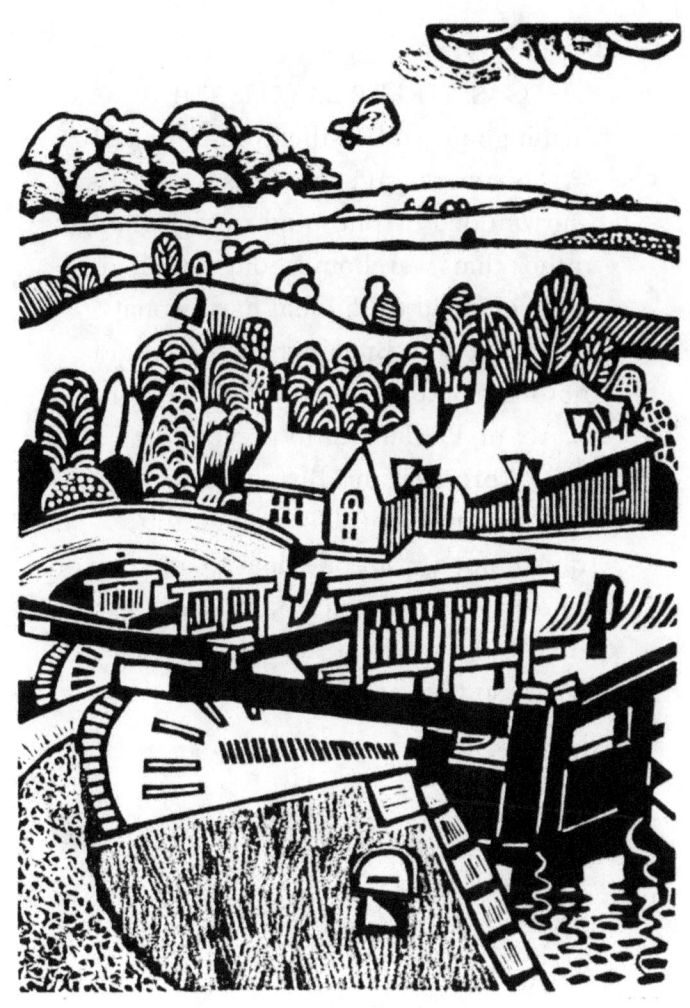

FOXTON STAIRCASE

GAS STREET BASIN IS THE Birmingham end of the Worcester and Birmingham canal. It is now surrounded by pubs and restaurants rather than warehouses, but still filled with colourful traditional narrowboats. The influential Birmingham Canal did not like competitors so it obtained an Act of Parliament to prevent the Worcester and Birmingham connecting to it. Goods had to be transshipped from one boat to another across the 'Worcester Bar'. This was finally pierced by a stop lock in 1815 so that boats could pass.

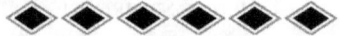

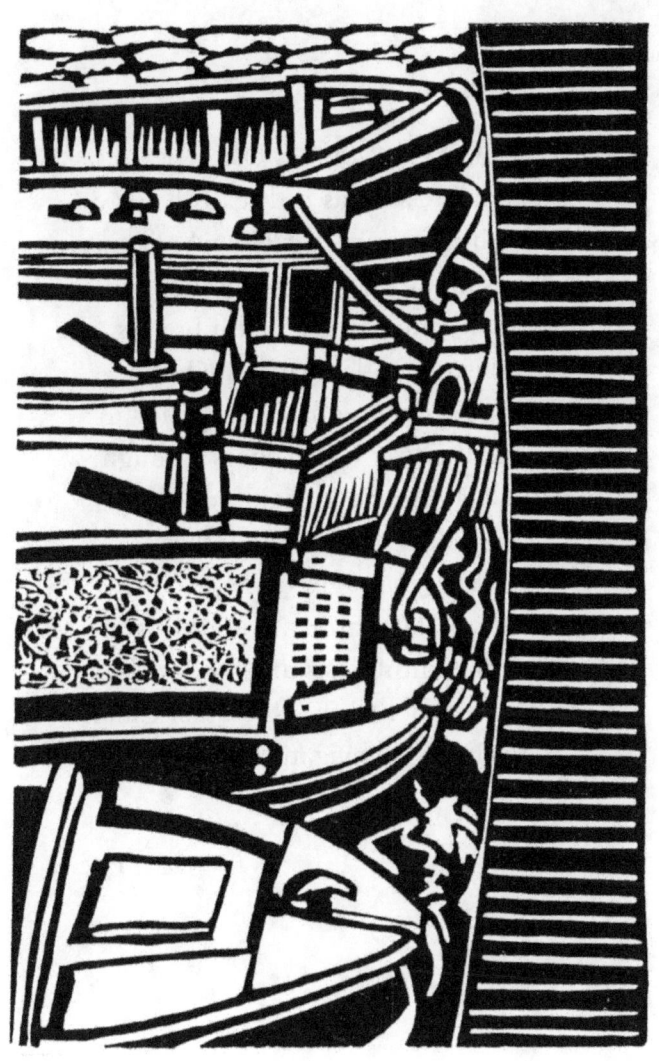

GAS STREET BASIN

LOOKING DOWN ON THE
Rochdale Canal as it threads its way
through the crowded Calder Valley at
Gauxholme near Todmorden. The
narrow valley is filled with houses,
industry, roads, river, canal and
George Stephenson's Manchester to
Leeds Railway which slices through
the chaos on an elegant, long and
curving viaduct. The railway
eventually brought closure to the
canal, the last through cargo was in
1937, but enthusiasts and Millennium
millions reopened the Rochdale Canal
to through navigation in 2002.

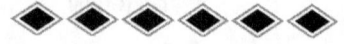

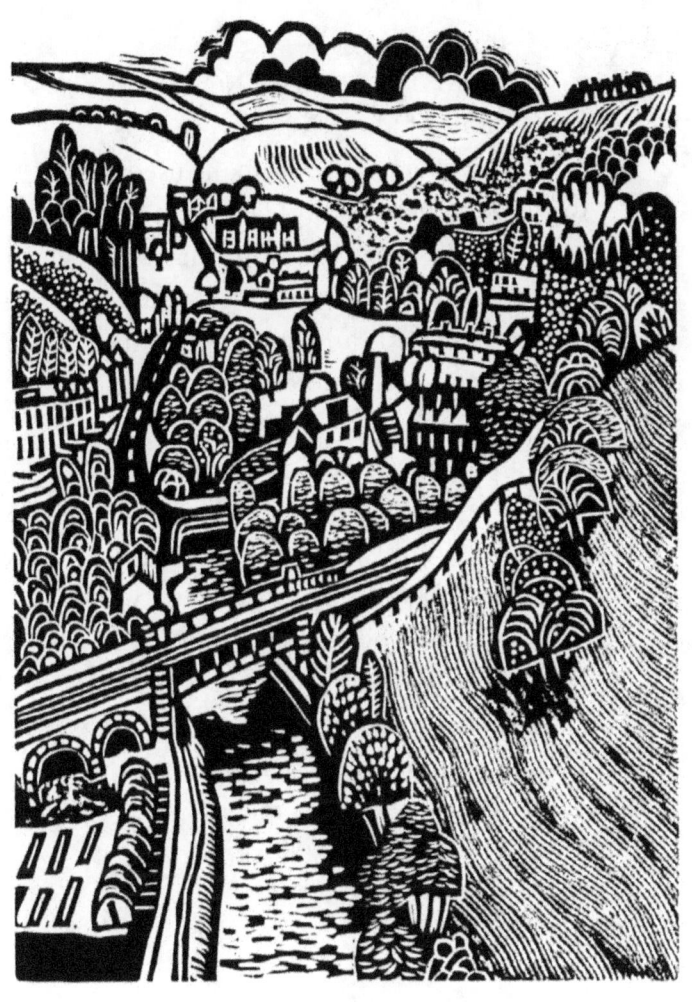

GAUXHOLME, TODMORDEN

GLOUCESTER, AT THE NORMAL
tidal limit of the River Severn, has
been a port since the Romans used it
to support their Welsh Campaigns. In
1793 a 25.7km [16mls] ship canal to
Berkeley Pill was started to bypass
dangerous bends and shallows on the
river. Costs were underestimated and it
only opened in 1823 using public loans.
Traffic boomed and the Victorian
docks and warehouse facilities
expanded until 1852 when the last
warehouse, Llanthony Warehouse, was
built. It now houses the National
Waterways Museum Gloucester, the
rest of the docks having been
converted to an attractive visitor
attraction with shops, offices and a
working dry dock.

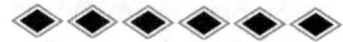

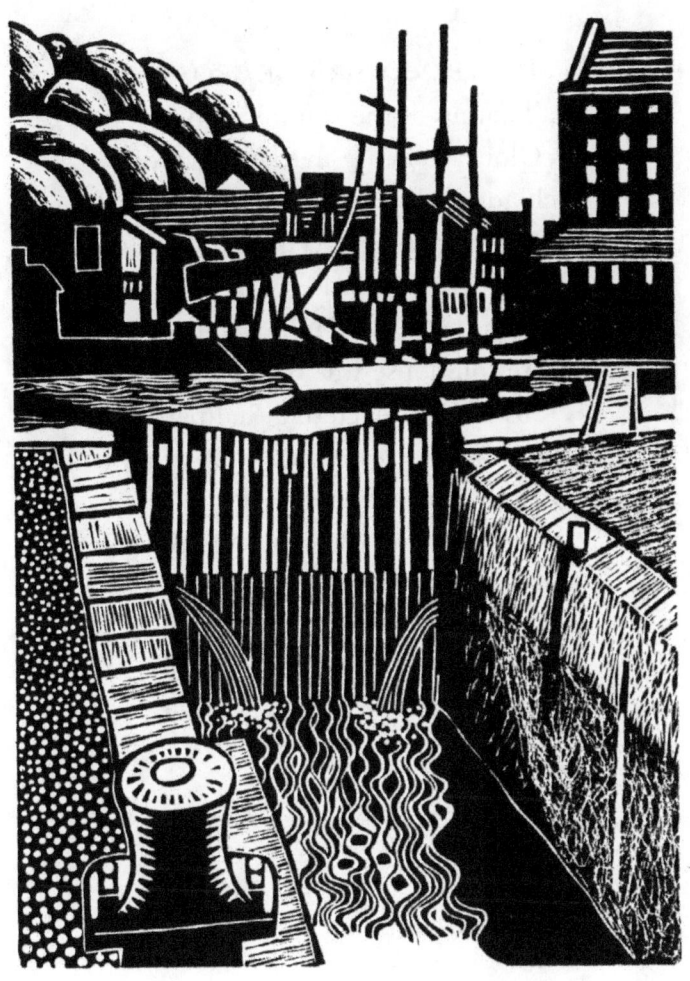

GLOUCESTER DOCKS

41

HALFPENNY BRIDGE CROSSES
the Thames at the southern end of the
Gloucestershire market town of
Lechlade. It has three arches, the main
one spanning the river, and was built
of beautiful Cotswold stone in 1792 to
a design by James Hollingworth. The
square toll house was built to allow the
tolls to be collected, a 'halfpenny'
being the rate for pedestrians when it
was opened. The toll was abolished
as long ago as 1839, but the name
lingers on!

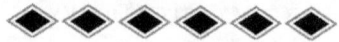

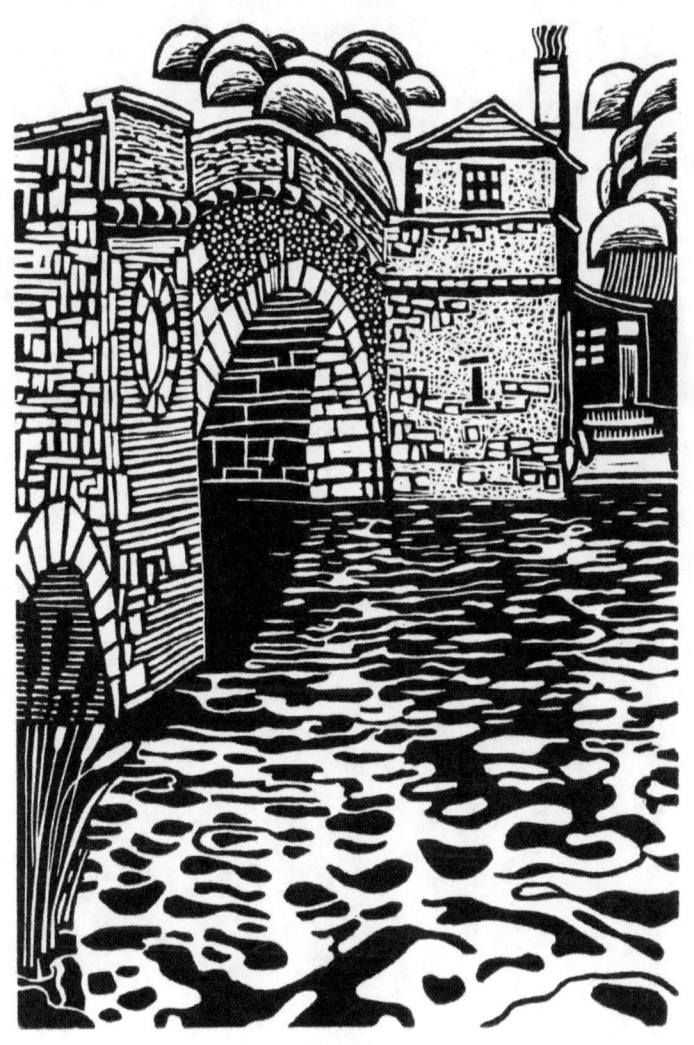

HALFPENNY BRIDGE AT LECHLADE

THE FLIGHT OF 21 BROAD LOCKS
at Hatton on the Grand Union canal
was opened by the Duke of Kent in
1934. Their construction was part of a
last gasp effort, backed by the
government of the day, to modernize
the canals so they could compete with
road and rail. It took two years and
1000 men to build the locks, using the
new material, concrete. The flight is a
daunting sight for boaters who
nicknamed the locks 'the stairway to
heaven'. The famous mechanical
paddle gear make winding easy
but slow.

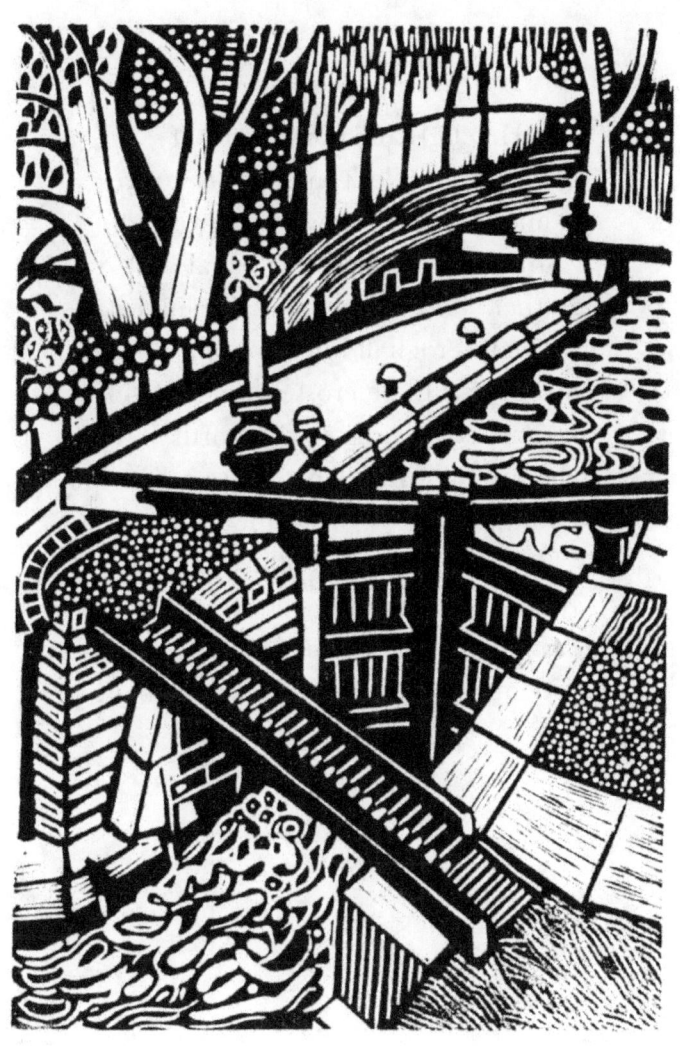

HATTON FLIGHT, TOP LOCK

HAZLEHURST AQUEDUCT,
(or Denford) built in 1841, is a rare
example of a waterways 'flyover', an
aqueduct carrying one canal over
another. The Caldon Canal splits with
the main Froghall line dropping down
three locks to be crossed by the Leek
branch as it swings to the north. This
unusual arrangement is to take
advantage of the shape of the
Churnet Valley. The fine, massive
brick arch is ornately decorated and
engraved, although some say the
stonemason did misspell 'Hazelhurst'!

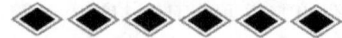

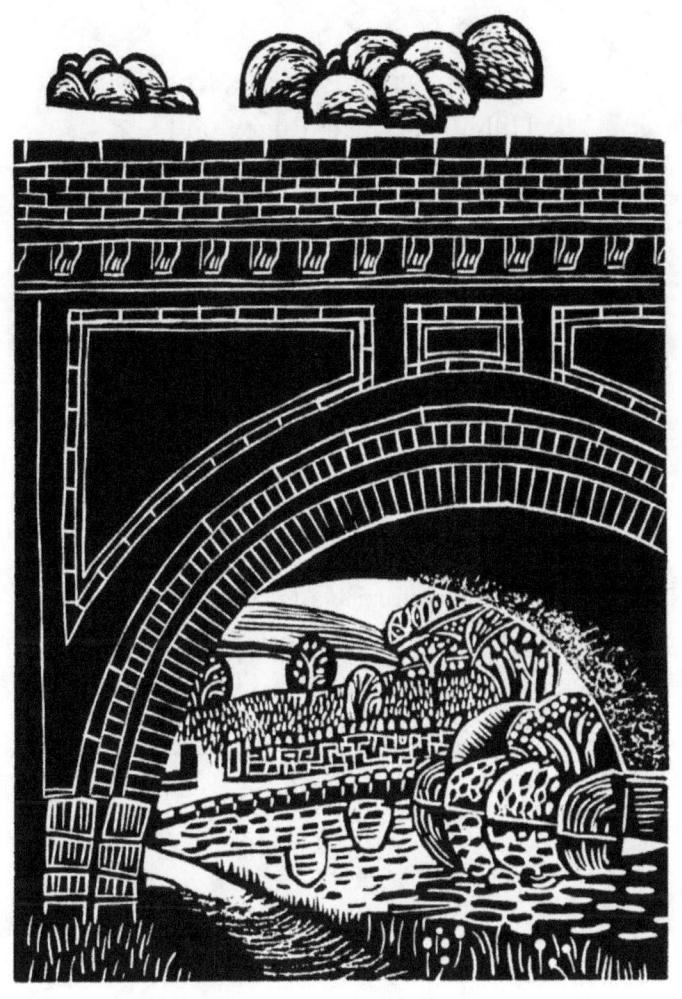

HAZLEHURST AQUEDUCT

THE THREE LOCKS AT
Hillmorton near Rugby on the
125.5km[77mls] Oxford Canal were
duplicated in 1840 to reduce waiting
times, part of the modernization of
the canal. This work also cut out
numerous loops in the canal reducing
its length by 22.5km[14mls]. 'Paired'
locks were very popular with boat
people who were working the
traditional motor boat and butty 'pair'
since both could be locked at the same
time. The Oxford Canal was busy and
profitable carrying Warwickshire coal
and other goods to the Thames and
London right up until nationalization
in 1946.

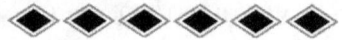

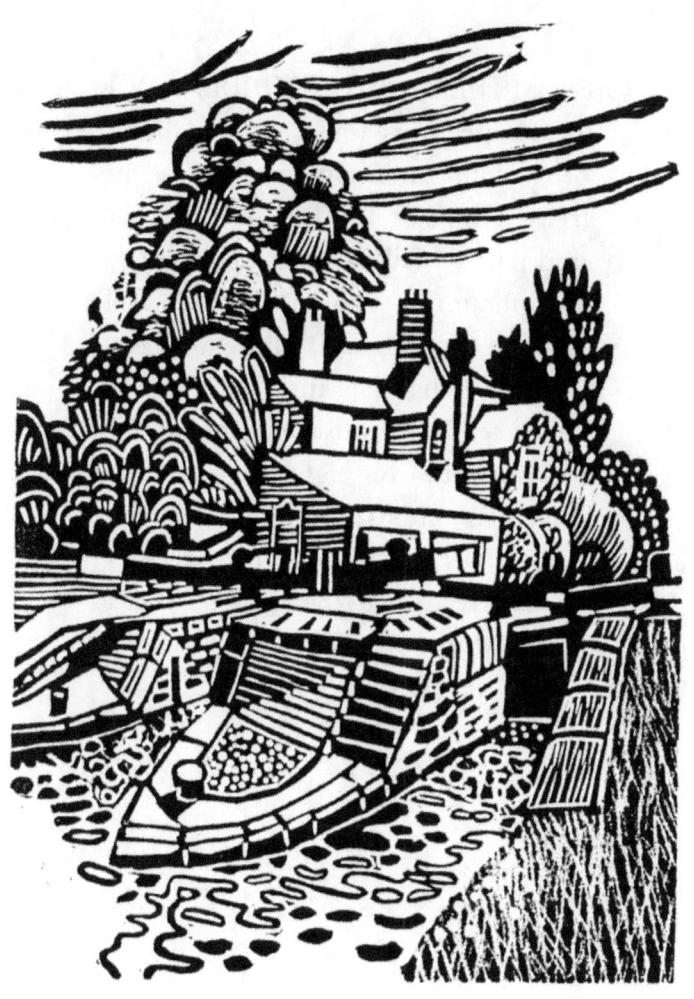

HILLMORTON BOTTOM LOCKS

FROM HILLMORTON MIDDLE LOCK the 16th century tower of the Church of St. John the Baptist peeks over the trees. The church overlooks the canal and part of Hillmorton, which was a combination of two settlements; 'Hill' was on the hill, and 'Moor' was the lower lying! The three locks are consistently the busiest on the canal network with over eight thousand boat movements in 2021. It's often claimed that canals are 'busier now than they ever were …'. In 1840 20,859 boats passed through Hillmorton locks!

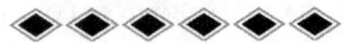

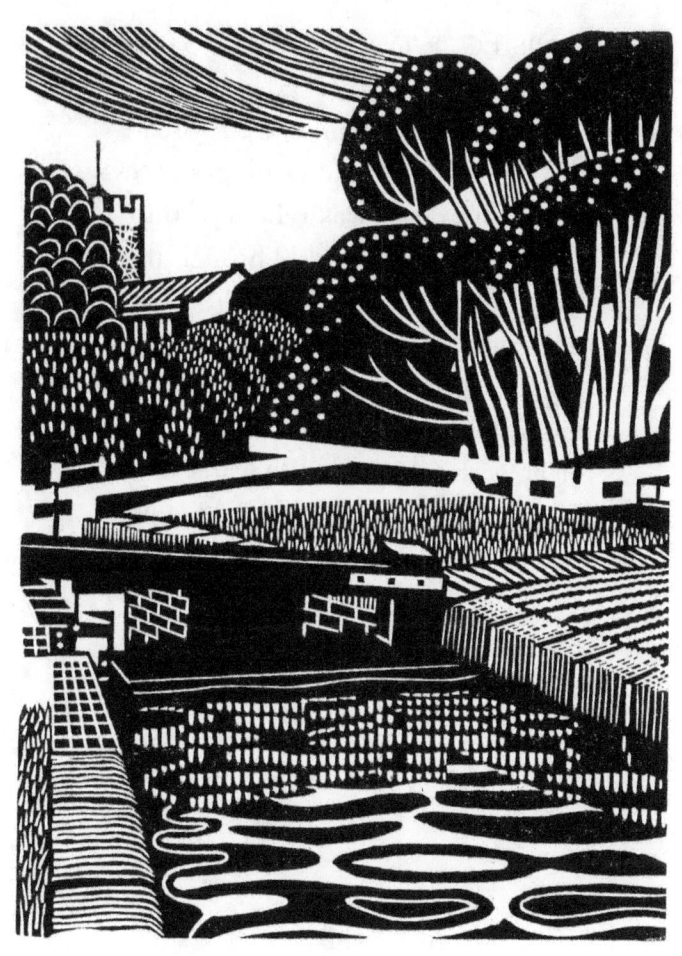

HILLMORTON MIDDLE LOCKS

ISIS LOCK IN OXFORD SITS ON
a short link from the Oxford Canal to
the upper River Thames. A broad
1797 lock gave Thames barges access
to Oxford but was rebuilt as this
narrow lock in 1844. Through the
bridge the canal heads north, a sharp
right turn taking boats to the current
terminus near Nuffield College. Below
the lock Castle Mill Stream joins the
Sheepwash Channel, a bywater of the
Thames. A railway swing bridge here
had to be wound open by hand to let
boats through.

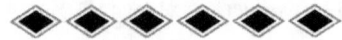

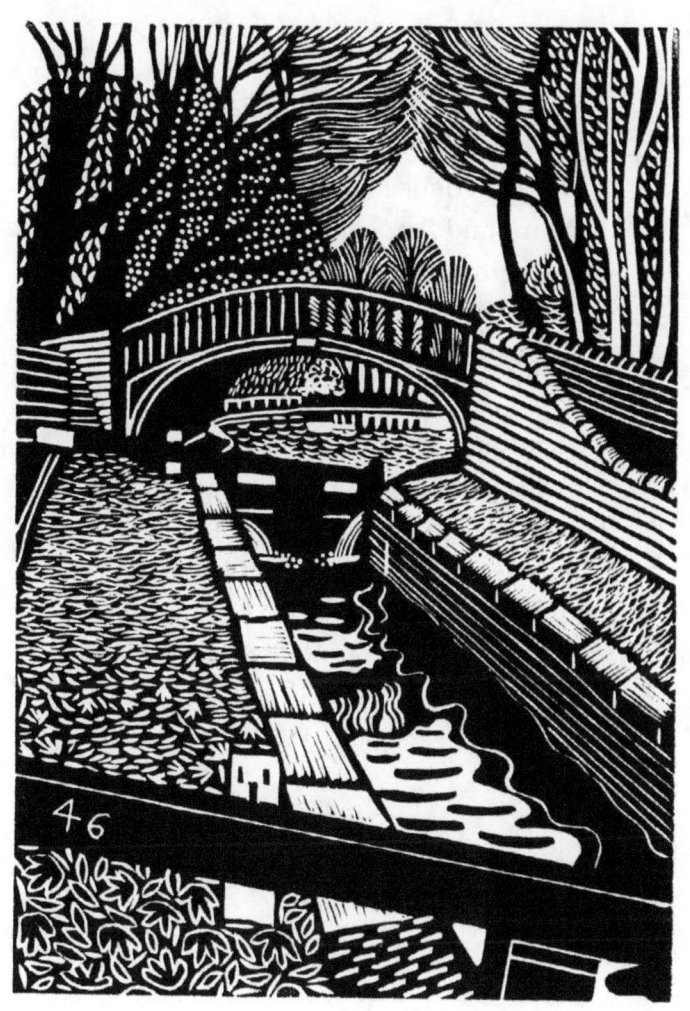

ISIS LOCK, OXFORD

KIDDERMINSTER LOCK ON
the Staffordshire and Worcestershire
canal is overlooked by the spectacular St.
Mary and All Saints parish church,
dating from the 15th and 16th century.
The 'Staffs and Worcs.' as it is popularly
known was an early 'contour' canal.
Opened in 1772 it was part of Brindley's
intention to create a 'Grand Cross' of
canals connecting the rivers Severn and
Trent, and the Mersey and Thames. The
canal was still making a profit when it
was nationalized in 1948, having been
run from the same Wolverhampton
offices for over 170 years!

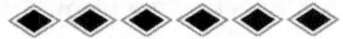

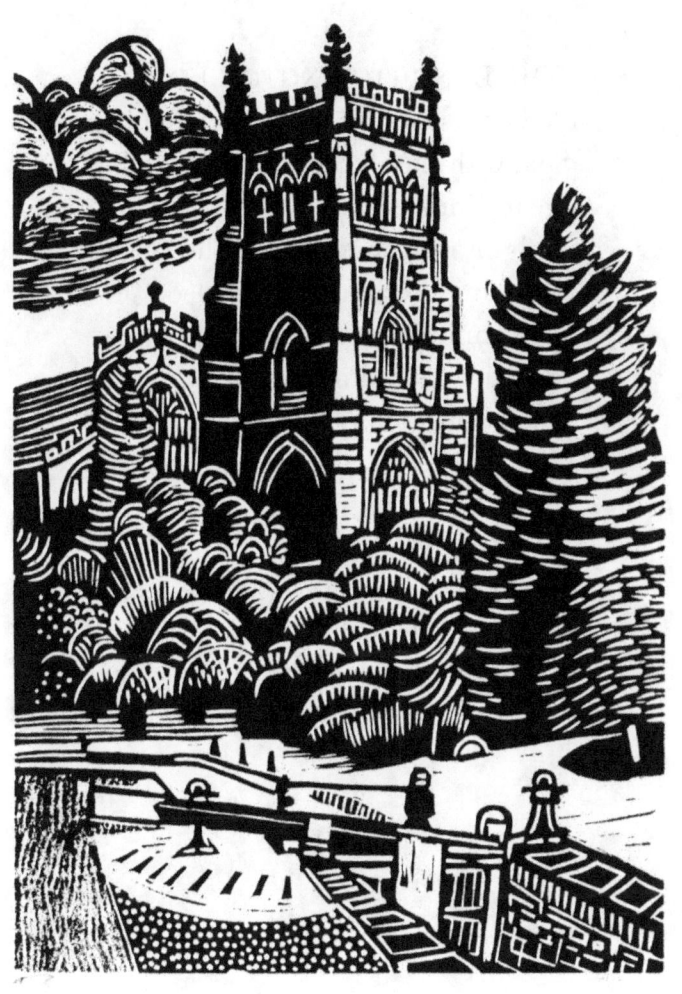

KIDDERMINSTER CHURCH

THE LONG ITCHINGTON LOCKS, a few miles west of Royal Leamington Spa, with their characteristic paddle gear. These locks form part of the climb into Birmingham on the Grand Union Canal. The angled mechanically geared paddles were introduced as part of the modernization of the canal in the 1930's. Most canals have one summit level, the Grand Union has two. It climbs from the River Thames at Brentford up into the Chiltern hills, descends, then climbs again to the Birmingham summit level, over 180 locks in all.

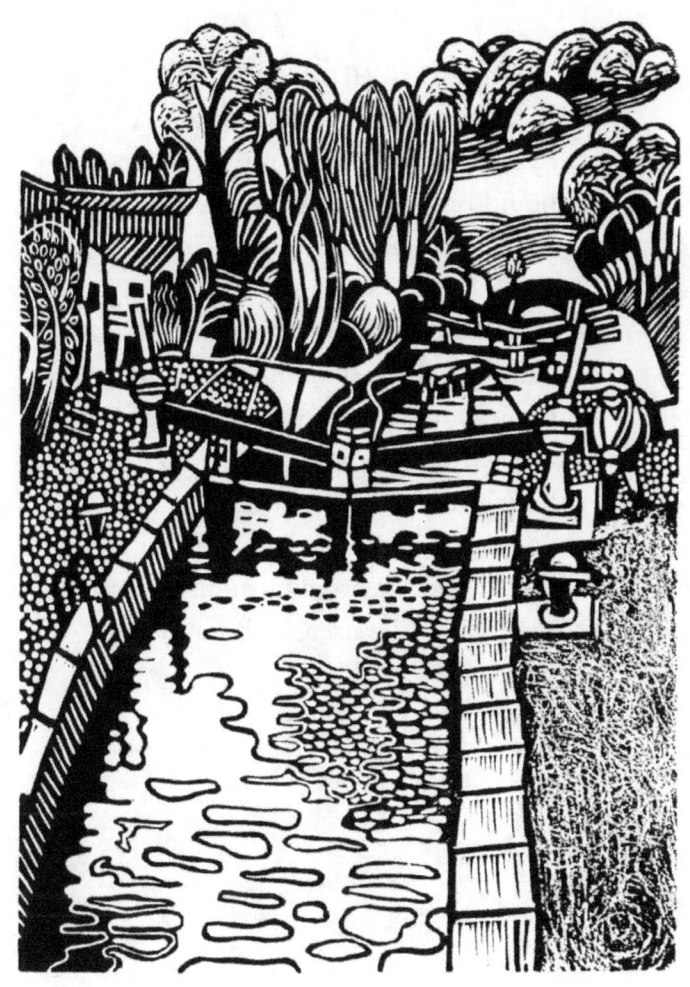

LONG ITCHINGTON FLIGHT

LUDGATE BRIDGE OVER THE 'Old Thirteen' on the Birmingham & Fazeley Canal sits surrounded by bland brick buildings. But follow Ludgate Hill up to find the exquisite 1779 St Paul's church, sitting in Birmingham's only tree lined Georgian Square in the fascinating Jewellery Quarter. The church and square were funded by a local landowner to tempt the wealthy to build houses on his surrounding estate, but the coming of the canal quickly brought industry and commerce to the area and scuppered his plans!

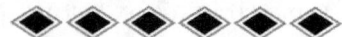

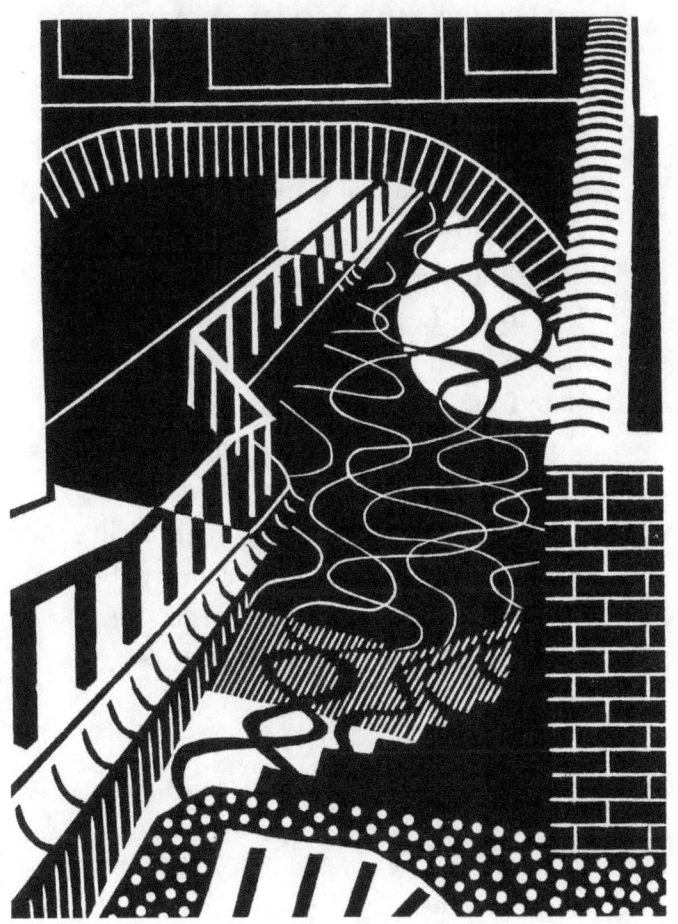

LUDGATE BRIDGE, BIRMINGHAM

MATHER MILL SITS ALONGSIDE
the Leigh Branch of the Bridgewater
Canal which was opened in 1799 as
part of the Duke of Bridgewater's
schemes to control transport between
Manchester and Liverpool. However
he did not see the opening of the final
link to the Leeds and Liverpool canal
in Wigan in 1820. The mill buildings
date from about the same period, the
lower building was the carding shed
sitting parallel to the canal but set at
an angle to the four storey main mill
building. In the nineteenth century the
skyline of Leigh was a panorama of
cotton mills and smoking chimneys.

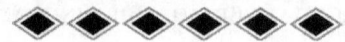

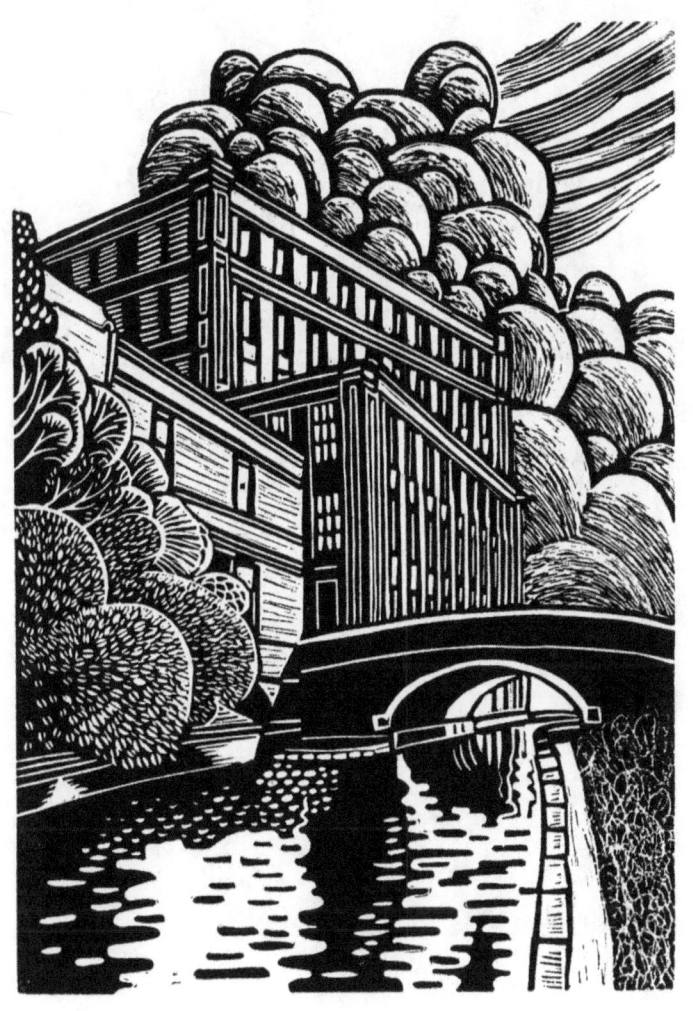

MATHER MILL, LEIGH BRANCH

IN 1889 BURLEIGH POTTERY
moved into its 'state of the art'
Middleport works alongside the Trent
and Mersey Canal in Burslem, Stoke
on Trent. Of its seven 'bottle kilns', so
called because of the distinctive shape,
only one remains, narrowly saved from
demolition in 1982, once over 2000
stood in the Potteries. The pottery
itself was narrowly saved from closure
in 2011 by the Prince's Regeneration
Trust raising £9m to restore the
buildings and create a visitor centre
still producing the world famous
Burleigh ware.

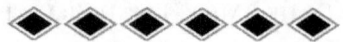

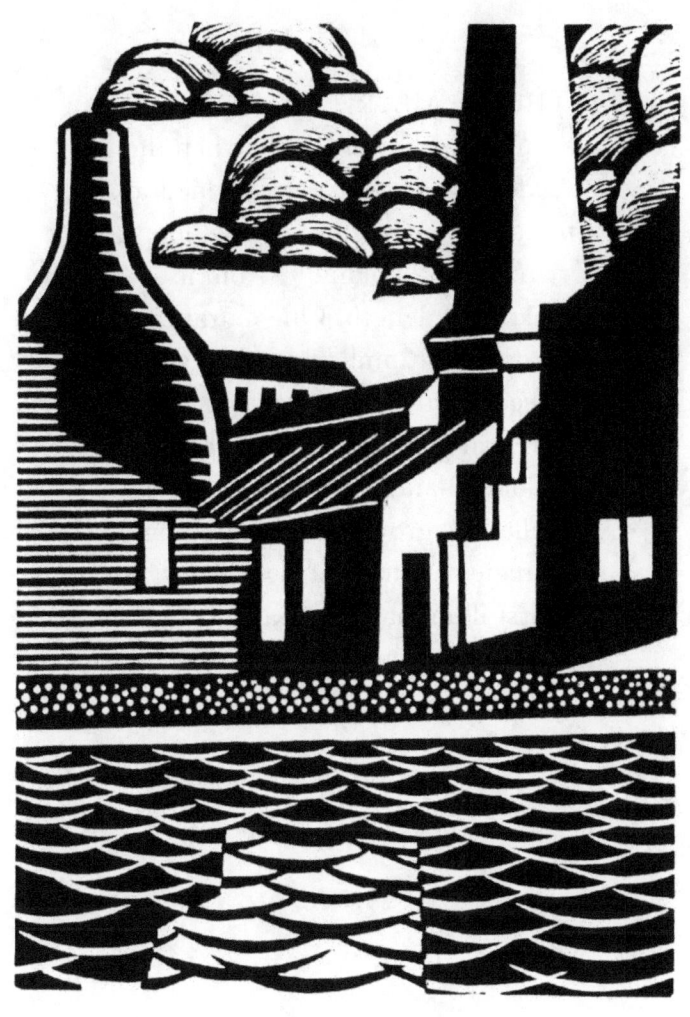

MIDDLEPORT POTTERY

THE 250 METRE[820FT] NEWBOLD tunnel was built in 1829 when the Oxford Canal was straightened to remove many of the original loops, cutting 22.5km[14mls] from its 146km[91mls] length. One entrance to the original 125m[410ft] tunnel can still be seen in the nearby St. Botolph's churchyard. In 2005 Rugby Borough Council and British Waterways installed 10 groups of coloured lights to create a 'tunnel of light' effect. It was first illuminated as part of Rugby's 'Diwali', the Hindu Festival of Lights.

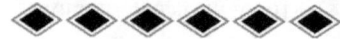

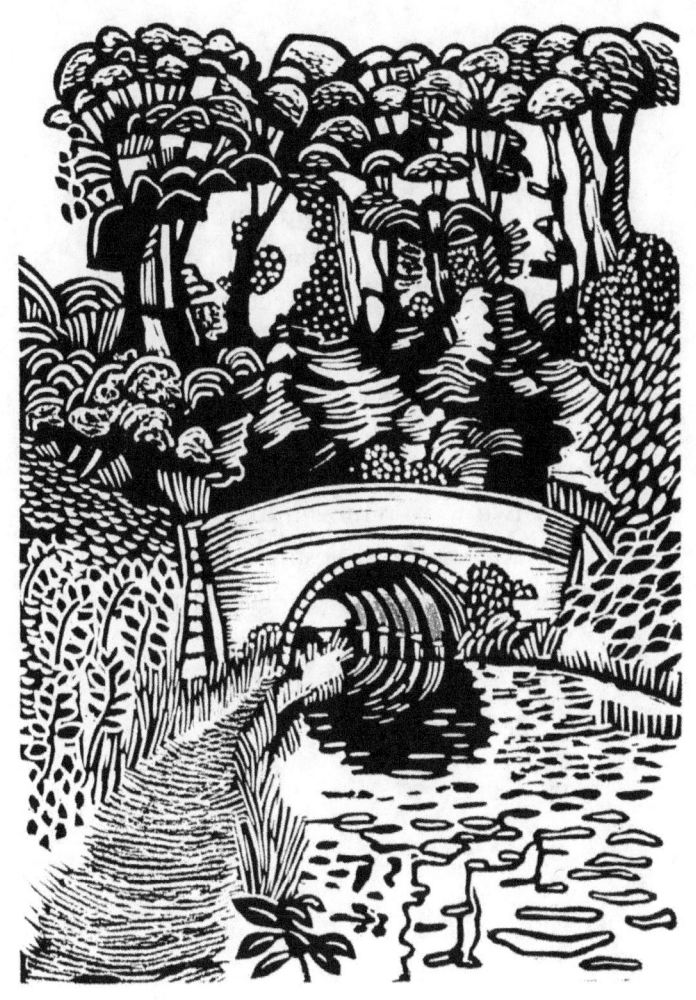

NEWBOLD TUNNEL

NORTHGATE LOCKS ON THE
Shropshire Union Canal at Chester
are a staircase of three broad locks,
sharing top and bottom gates.
Staircase locks were used to climb
steeply, and were more economical to
build than single locks. The locks fall
10m[33ft]. Originally there were five
locks in the staircase lowering almost
to the level of the River Dee, but the
lower two were removed in 1797 when
the extension to Ellesmere Port was
opened. The railway bridge carries the
North Wales mainline to Holyhead
and the old GWR mainline to
Shrewsbury and Birmingham.

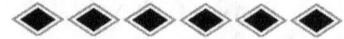

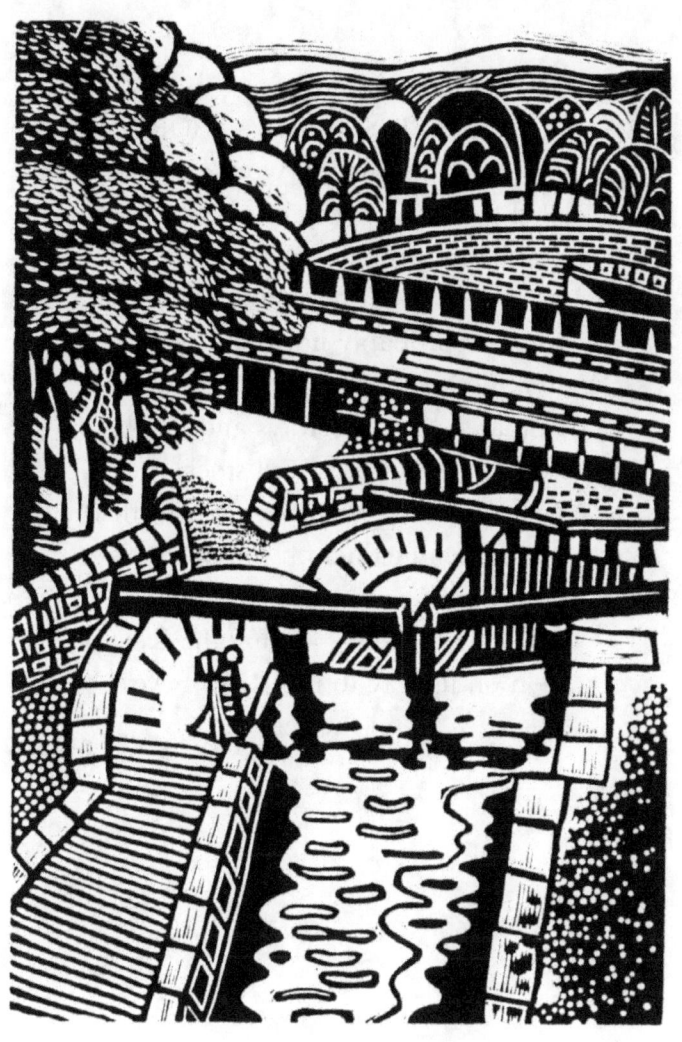

NORTHGATE LOCKS, CHESTER

THE RIVER SWIFT IS A SHORT tributary of the River Avon, originally called the 'Lutre' which means 'sweet stream', and probably gave its name to Lutterworth built on its banks. These days it is probably not that 'sweet' a stream, passing through a landscape dominated by motorways and derelict railway lines, but it is well stocked with coarse fish and does flow beneath this fine brick aqueduct on the northern Oxford Canal close to Rugby, immediately before joining the River Avon on its way to the River Severn and the sea.

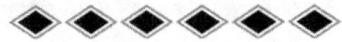

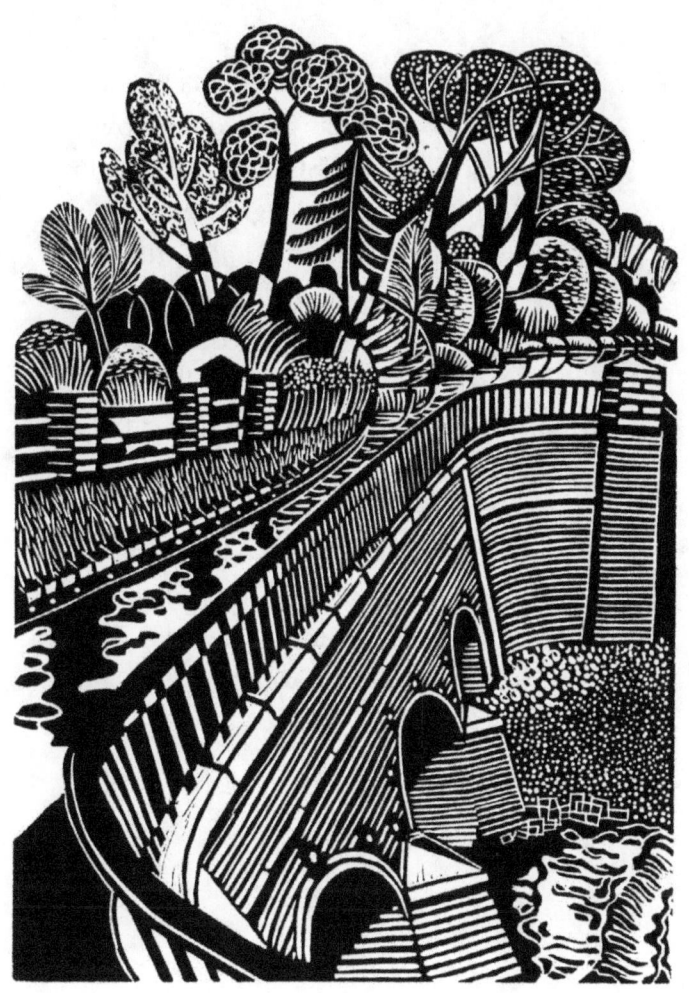

OXFORD CANAL OVER RIVER SWIFT, RUGBY

TOWERING ABOVE THE RIVER
Dee is the Pontcysyllte Aqueduct, now
recognized by UNESCO as a World
Heritage Site. A 'magnificent
masterpiece of the canal age', the
307m[1007ft] long, 38.5m[126ft] tall, 19
arch aqueduct was completed in 1805,
the inspirational work of William
Jessop and Thomas Telford. The canal
is carried in a cast iron trough, made
of dovetailed sections, sealed with
Welsh flannel dipped in boiling sugar
and molten lead. The trough sits on
tapered stone piers, hollow towards the
top to reduce weight.

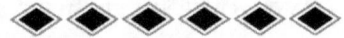

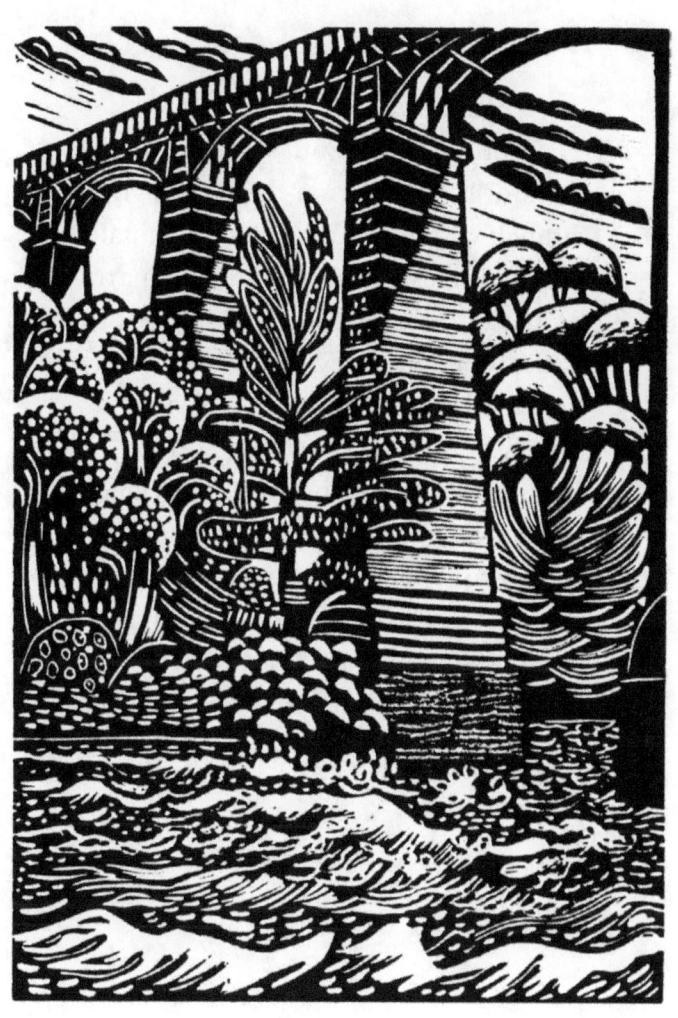

PONTCYSYLLTE AQUEDUCT

BRIDGE 28A IN CAMDEN.

The Regent's Canal was only 13.8km[8.6mls] long from the Paddington branch of the Grand Junction Canal down 12 locks to the Thames. A part of master architect John Nash's 1811 North London redevelopment plans it carried the blessing of the Prince Regent. However there were construction problems, water shortages and then money shortages after the Superintendent, Thomas Horner, disappeared with a large amount of investors' money. Government unemployment relief funds completed the canal in 1820.

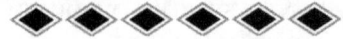

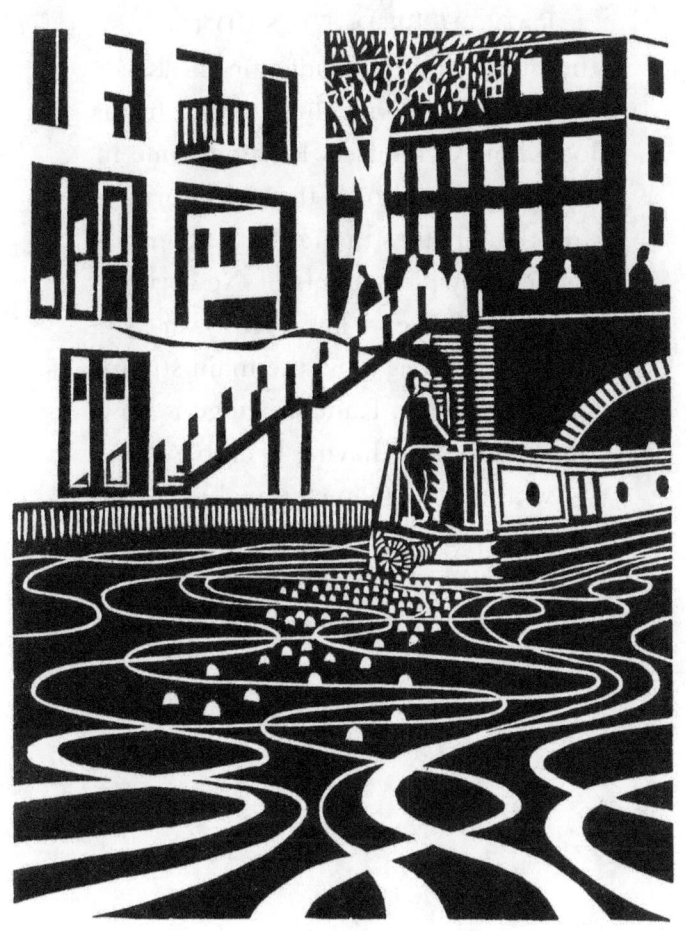

REGENTS CANAL

RADCOT BRIDGE IS SAID TO BE
the most beautiful bridge on the River
Thames, built with three arches from
local honey coloured Taynton stone in
1200. It may also be the oldest bridge
on the Thames though that claim is
disputed by proponents of Newbridge,
built 50 years later. However
Newbridge does cross the main stream
of the Thames, Radcot Bridge is now
on a backwater, having been bypassed
by a 'new cut' opened in 1787 to
improve navigation. Radcot Bridge
also had to be substantially rebuilt
after damage in battles in the 14th and
15th centuries, its previously pointed
centre arch being levelled.

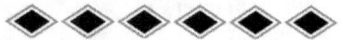

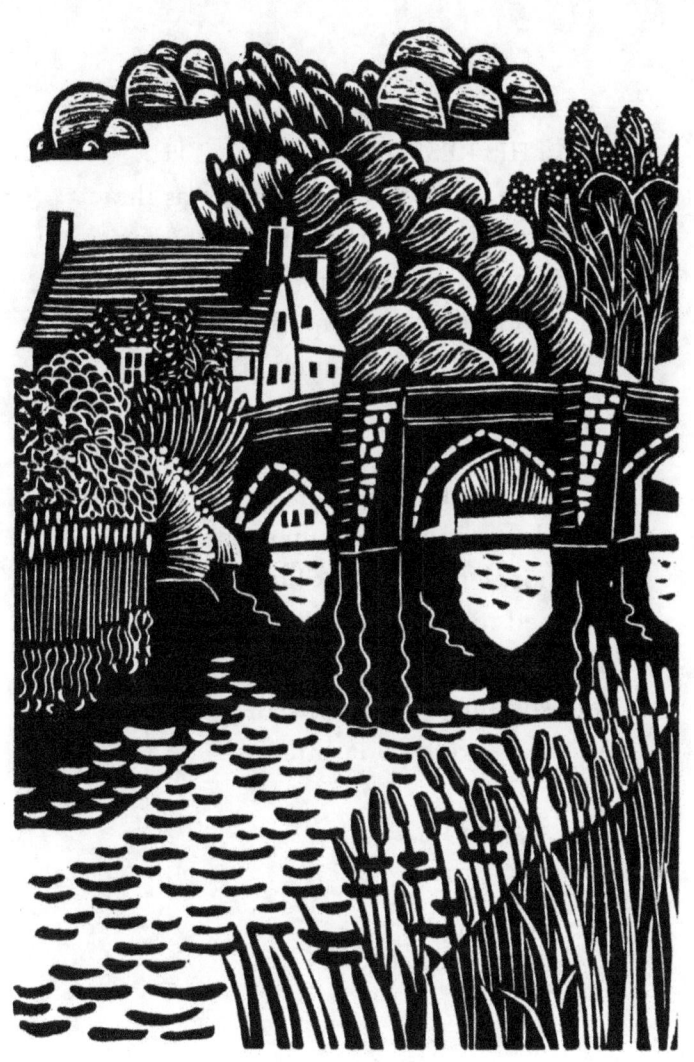

RADCOT, THE THAMES

THIS RESTORED LOCK BY THE
River Irwell in Manchester was the
entrance to the long lost Manchester &
Salford Junction Canal which ran for
just over 800m[0.5mls], mostly beneath the
city streets, to a junction with the
Rochdale Canal. The canal was opened
in 1839 but it was expensive to build
and maintain with a 500m[0.3mls] tunnel,
four locks and 2 pumping stations on its
short length. It was little used and
closed to through traffic just 36 years
later. Some of the underground sections
are still intact, including that under the
Granada Studios.

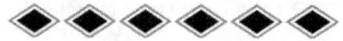

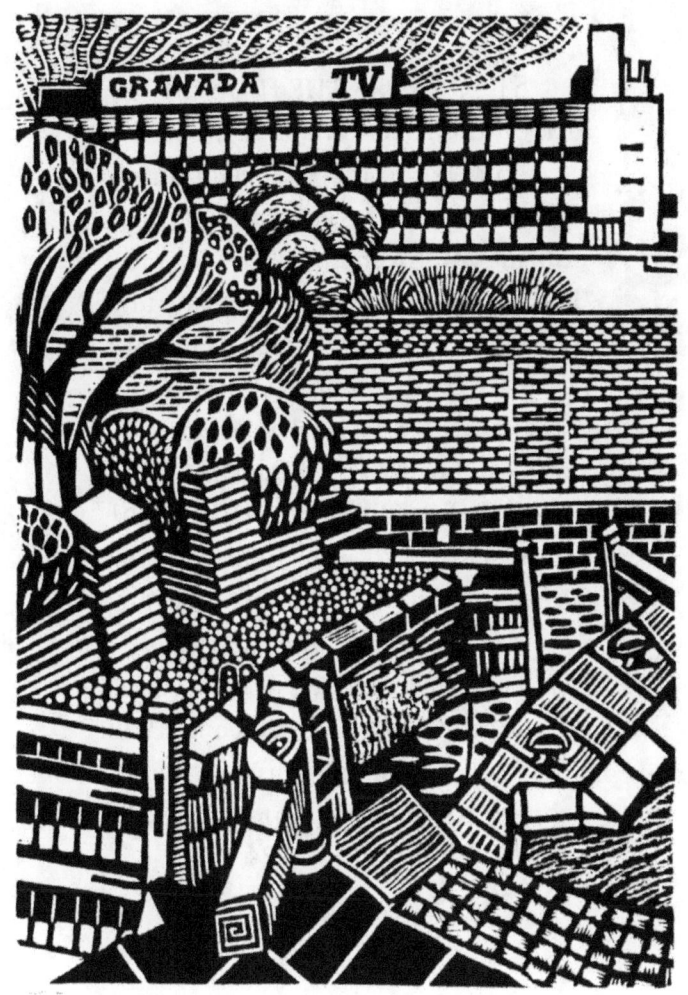

RIVER IRWELL LOCK

St John's is the highest
lock on the River Thames, the first of
45 down to the tidal river at
Teddington. It was built in 1790
during improvements to the Upper
Thames to cope with the extra traffic
generated by the opening of Thames
and Severn canal. It retains its
distinctive manual wheel operated
paddles. The lock is the resting place
of 'Old Father Thames', a Portland
Cement statue commissioned for the
Great Exhibition at Crystal Palace in
1854. Father Thames has led a
charmed life, rescued from the fire
that destroyed Crystal Palace in 1936,
then saved from vandalism by being
brought to this most appropriate safe
location in 1974.

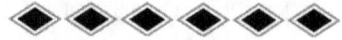

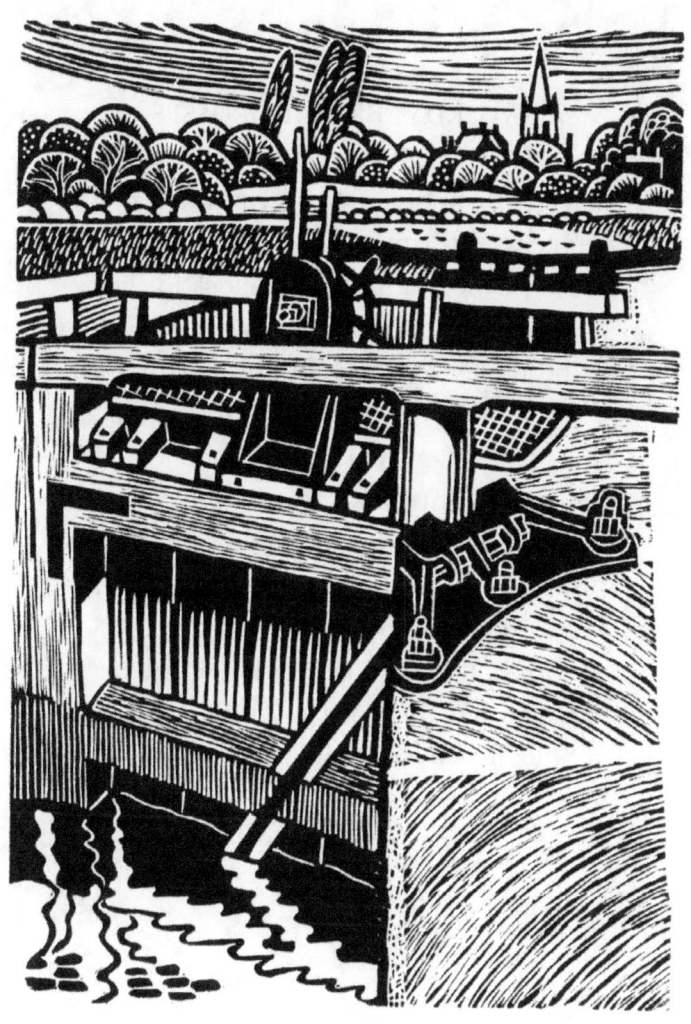

ST. JOHN'S LOCK, LECHLADE

SATURDAY BRIDGE CROSSES
the Farmers Bridge flight of 13 locks
on the Birmingham and Fazeley Canal
in central Birmingham. These cobbles
once echoed around the clock to the
sound of the hooves of the donkeys
and mules used to pull the short haul
'joey boats' along the 289km[180mls] of
canals which made up the
Birmingham Canal Navigations. The
imaginative regeneration of the
Birmingham canals and surroundings,
including the nearby ICC &
Symphony Hall and National Indoor
Arena, has turned this into a popular
walk for city workers and shoppers.

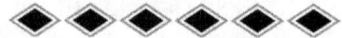

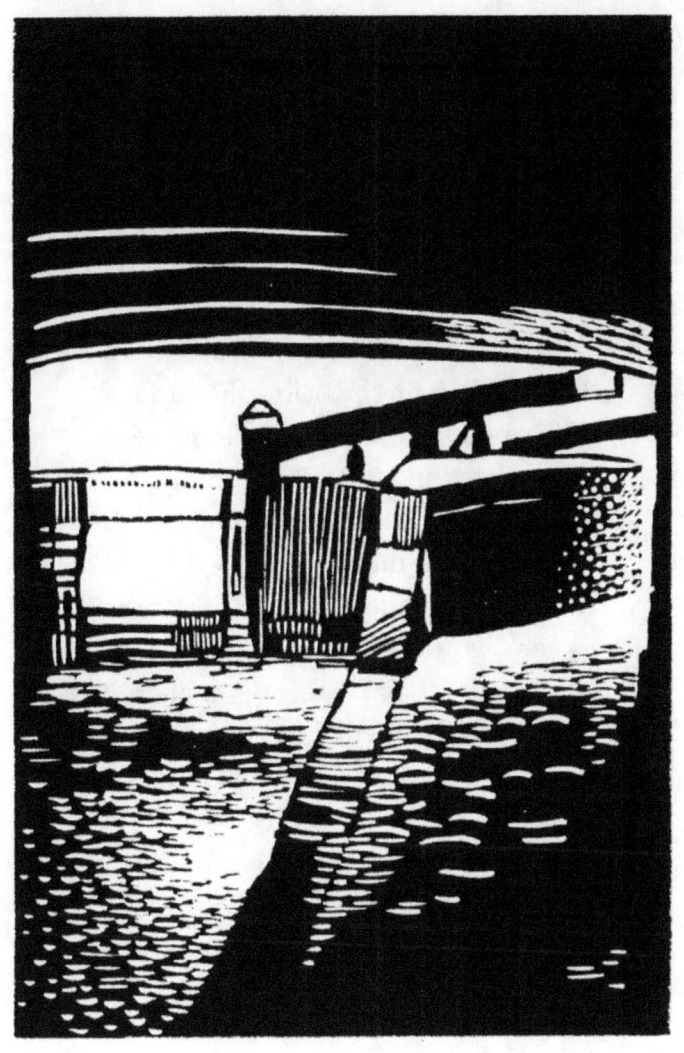

SATURDAY BRIDGE

STANDEDGE TUNNEL ON THE Huddersfield Narrow Canal is the longest, deepest and highest canal tunnel in Britain. Cutting through the heart of the Pennines, the tunnel is 5.2km[3.2mls] long, 196m[643ft] above sea level and 194m[636ft] below the surface. Fifty men lost their lives before it was completed in 1811 after 17 years of hard physical labour. Major roof collapses in the tunnel closed it to through navigation in 1945 but after a year's worth of dredging and much structural repair costing £5 million it was reopened in 2001.

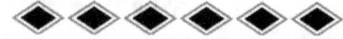

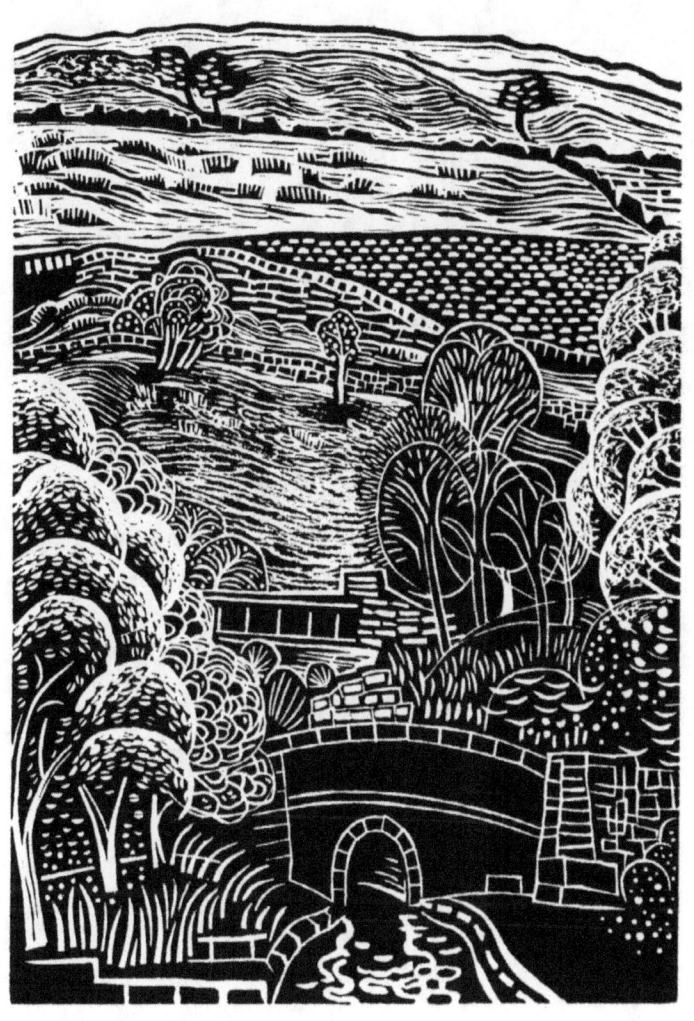

STANDEDGE TUNNEL

STOKE BRUERNE WAS A BUSY
village dating back to Roman times,
cut in half in 1800 when the Grand
Junction Canal was opened from
Braunston to the River Thames. It
prospered from the boatmen who
passed through, the two canalside pubs
being popular overnight resting places.
It now attracts tourists, to the famous
Canal Museum housed in a 200 year
old corn mill, canalside pubs and the
mile and three quarter long Blisworth
Tunnel which is just a short stroll
away. Many of the 'leggers' who
would push the boats through the
tunnel in the days before engines lived
in the village.

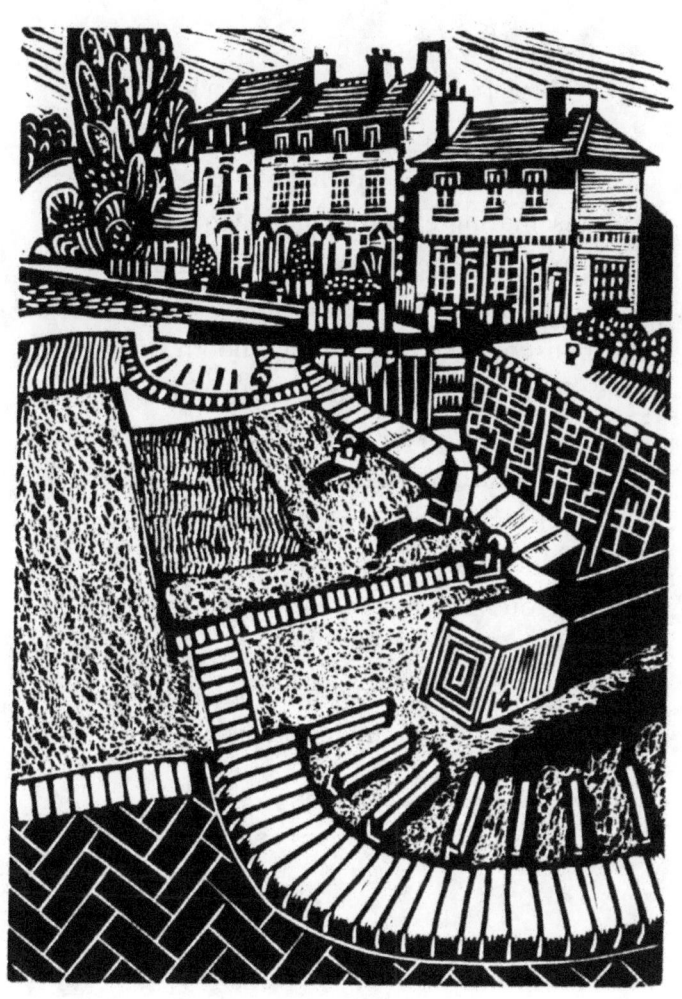

STOKE BRUERNE LOCK

STOURPORT, WHERE THE
Staffordshire & Worcestershire Canal
meets the River Severn, is a
fascinating example of a 'canal town',
possibly the only town in Britain to
have developed solely as a
consequence of the canal boom. It has
five interlinked basins, sets of broad
and narrow locks down to the river
and a fascinating collection of historic
buildings including warehouses, dry
dock and the magnificent Tontine
Hotel. An award winning heritage
project has revitalized the area,
restoring many buildings and
reopening the infilled Lichfield Basin.

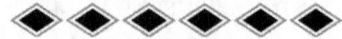

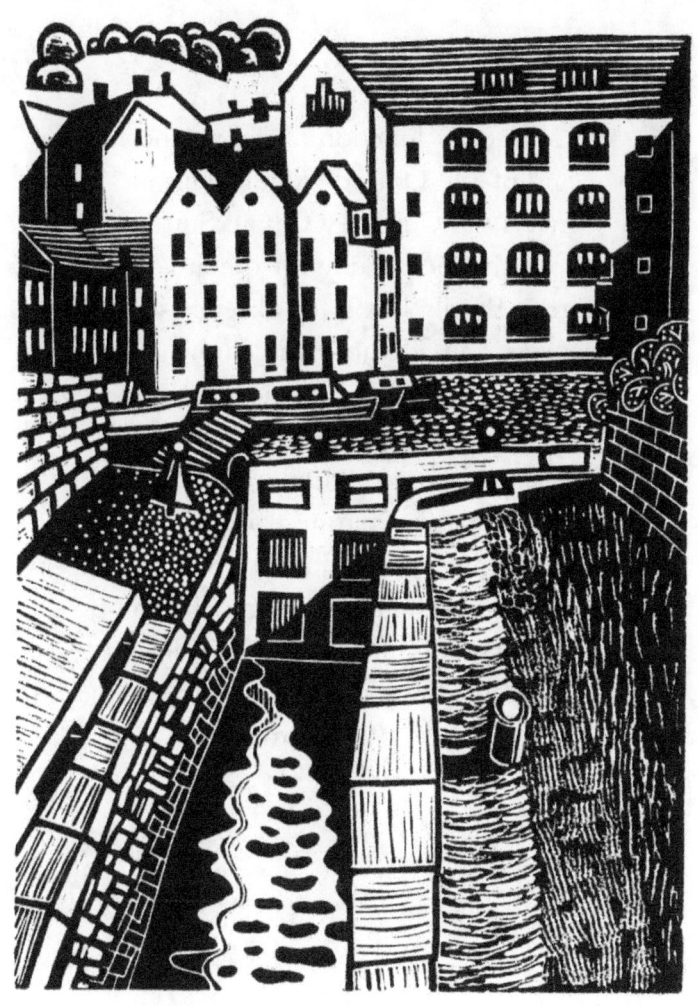

STOURPORT BASIN

SUTTON STOP LOCK IS AT
Hawkesbury Junction at the northern
end of the Oxford Canal where it
meets the Coventry Canal. Sutton
Stop is the local name for the area, the
Sutton Family being lock keepers here
for over half of the 19th century. The
shallow stop lock was not used to
lower the canal but to keep the water
belonging to the Oxford Canal
Company separate from that
belonging to the Coventry Canal
Company. The interesting collection
of waterway buildings and the elegant
cast iron bridge now form part of a
conservation area.

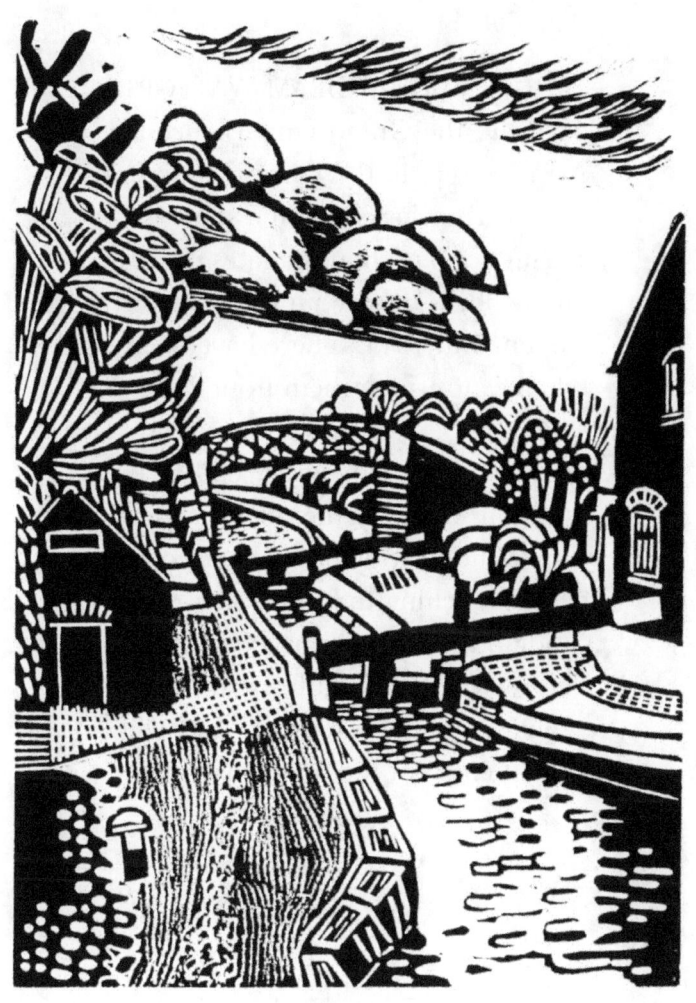

SUTTON STOP

THE 7 NARROW BEAM WATFORD
locks lift the Grand Union Leicester
Arm 16m[52ft] to the Leicester summit
level. Four locks are in a staircase
sharing top and bottom gates. Built as
narrow locks to save money, they were
opened in 1814. There have been
schemes to widen them from 2.1m[7ft]
to 4.2m[14ft] ever since. They, with
Foxton Locks at the other end of the
summit level, are the main barriers
preventing wide beam boats and
barges reaching the waterways of the
midlands and north from the broad
waterways of the south. If the Foxton
Inclined Plane is restored they will
then form the only barrier.

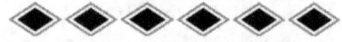

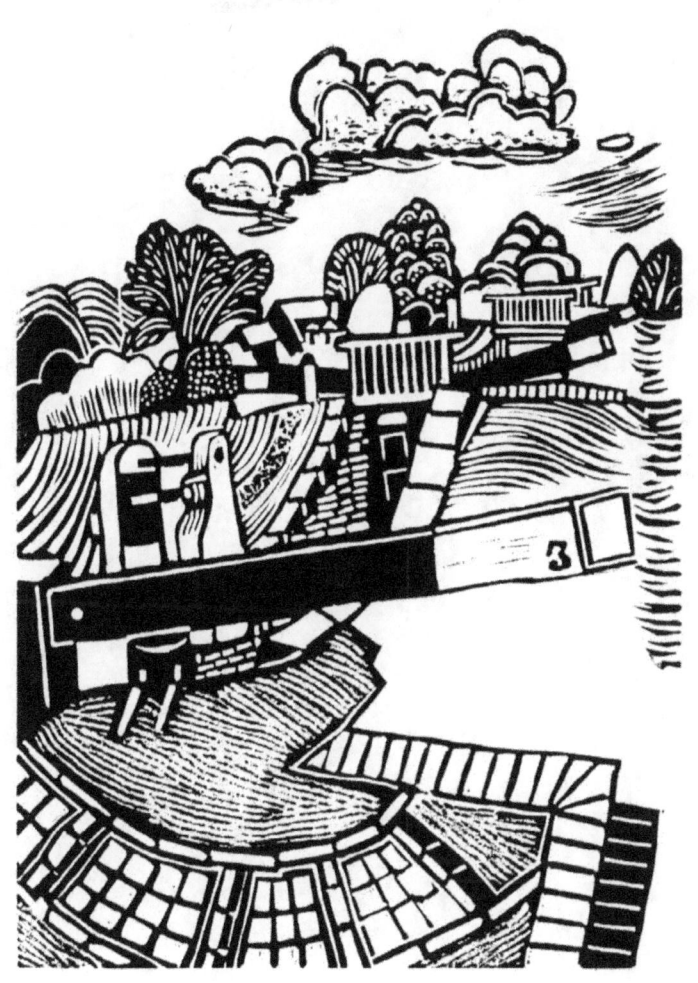

WATFORD STAIRCASE

 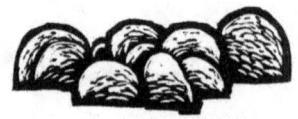

Eric Gaskell

Studied painting and printmaking at Wigan College and Sunderland University. He left art college in 1980 winning two painting scholarships, one to New York and one to Istanbul, as well as the Sunderland Fine Art prize. He has exhibited widely in Britain, Europe and the USA.

Brought up near the Leeds-Liverpool canal, swimming, fishing and watching the coal barges chug past has helped to produce a series of printed works from all over the canal system, but throwing a different light on the traditional canal drawing or painting.

Paul Higson

He created the popular Canal Junction website.